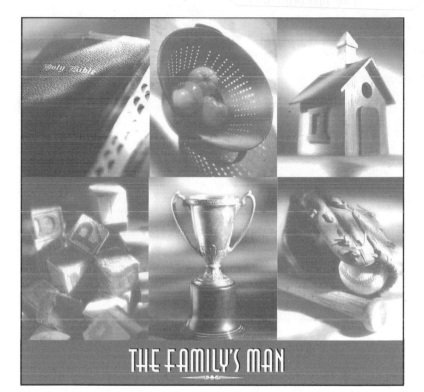

THE FAMILY'S MAN

THE FAMILY'S MAN
DEVOTIONS FOR MEN WHO LOVE THEIR FAMILIES

DANIEL PFAFFE

CPH.
SAINT LOUIS

Copyright © 2001 Daniel Pfaffe
Published by Concordia Publishing House
3558 S. Jefferson Avenue, St. Louis, MO 63118-3968
Manufactured in the United States of America

Library of Congress Cataloging-in-Publication Data

1 2 3 4 5 6 7 8 9 10   10 09 08 07 06 05 04 03 02 01

Acknowledgments

The great privilege to write this, my first written offering, goes with gratitude to the following:

The Triune God—the Father who created us, the Son by whose blood we are eternally saved, and the Holy Spirit who continues to keep us with Jesus Christ in the one true faith.

My wife, Debbie, who has honored me with her life, given me joy in mine, and whose love, encouragement, forgiveness, and patience—none of which I deserve—enabled me to see this project to completion.

My children, Mark, Andrew, Carissa, and Jonathan, who, at their tender age, have shown me their profound love, respect, patience, and proud support of "Daddy"—teaching me daily the joys of being my family's man.

My father and mother, Marvin and Dorothy Pfaffe, who introduced me to Jesus through the saving waters of Holy Baptism before I could even understand human speech. The Holy Spirit's work through their godly example and faithful worship attendance continues to feed my faith.

Norman Johnson, who encouraged me to begin writing this book and, with the help of his lovely wife, Pearl, reviewed the manuscript.

Robert Weidner and Steven Fisher, officers of my congregation at St. John's Lutheran Church and good friends, who also greatly assisted me in reviewing this manuscript.

The three congregations I serve—St. John's of Durand, Immanuel of Plum City, and St. Paul's of Canton Township, Wisconsin—who have never failed to express their love and respectful support, giving me great joy as their pastor.

The Durand Fire Department, 30 or so guys who keep my feet firmly planted on the ground (literally—I don't like heights!) and whose friendship I will value the rest of my life.

Dawn Weinstock, managing editor at Concordia Publishing House, who gave me the first indication I could take up writing a book seriously and provided the friendly cooperation and support I needed.

To God alone be the glory!

Foreword

What is a man? If you are a man reading this, you may feel fairly certain you know the answer to this question. If you are a woman reading this, you may have an opinion surprisingly different. Whoever you are, it is important to remember that the 21st-century world's definition of a man and what a man should do is radically different from previous definitions.

Since the advent of the feminist movement in the late sixties, the traditional roles assigned to men and women have been reconstructed. I am not concerned about "equal pay for equal work" or other issues in which men and women deserve to be treated fairly and equally. What concerns me is how our society has effectively taught men that women no longer need their support and companionship, even when children are involved.

God has much to say in His Word about His forgiving love for all people—men, women, and children alike. The greatest proof of His love for us is the gift of His only Son, Jesus, who died on the cross to pay for our sins in full. Trusting in God's dependable love inspires us to see the importance of our interdependence on one another. In His genius, God uses real life examples to teach us in concrete ways that we are totally dependent on Him: our dependence on our parents, our dependence on our wives, and even the dependence children and wives have on their fathers and husbands!

Therefore, the purpose of *The Family's Man* is to fill you with as much of God's Word as possible. By the power of God's Word, His Holy Spirit brings us to and keeps us in a saving faith in Jesus alone for the forgiveness of all our sins. That same Spirit of God enables us to live grateful lives pleasing to Him. With His aid, we will have fun exploring what it means to be the family's man. Whether you read the suggested Scripture readings at the beginning of each devotion or simply those imbedded in the meditation, it is my prayer that you will find God leading you to a richer understanding of His love for you, your wife, and your children.

Following the prayer after each meditation is a section titled "Today's Challenge" that applies the day's devotional thought to your daily living through action or reflection. If it seems a little strange at first, give it a week. I pray you'll find something in each devotion that you'll be able to hold on to throughout the day.

God bless each of you as you daily learn what it means to be members of His family—man, woman, and child—in Jesus' name! *To God alone be the glory!*

Daniel Pfaffe

TABLE OF CONTENTS

Part I

The Man of the Family

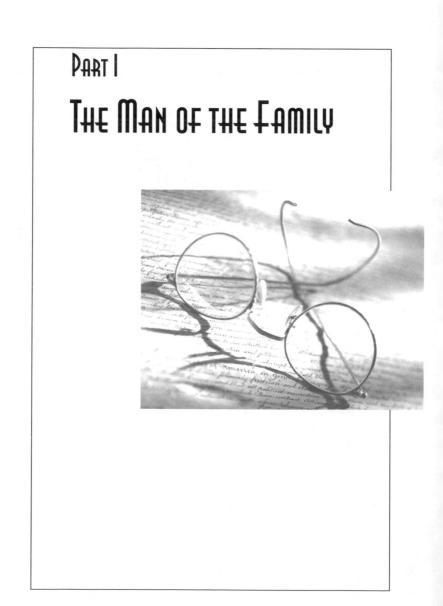

Read Psalm 2
Genesis 11:1–9

Making Your Name
Can Be Confusing

You can learn a lot walking through a graveyard. When I go to St. Louis, one of my favorite places to visit is Concordia Cemetery. I love to see the gravestones of those beloved leaders and teachers of faith. One may wonder why I don't spend my visit at the St. Louis Arch, Busch Stadium, or some other exciting attraction. Although the graveyard is not exciting, there is one thing the grave markers offer that the tourist attractions do not: a faith-strengthening Christian witness.

Many of these grave markers are statues of Jesus with features worn smooth over the decades. Bible passages are chiseled into granite, testifying to the need always to trust in Jesus alone for salvation. Even the less expensive gravestones bear a powerful Christian witness, such as the one that read, "Asleep in Jesus."

In contrast to these stones, other large monuments seem to be concerned only with reminding all who pass by that "Here lies _____." Whether in grave markers, houses, cars, boats, or other status symbols, our choices and purchases reflect the priorities we set in our lives. Who comes first, God or me? Whose name is greater in my life, God's or mine?

Genesis 11 shows the disastrous results that occur when people put their own names above God's. Before we look at chapter 11, remember what happened after Noah and his family got off the ark. In chapter nine, God told Noah and his sons, "Be fruitful and increase in number and fill the earth" (Genesis 9:1). As we read chapter 11, many years had passed. The generations following Noah were in the process of obeying this command:

> Now the whole world had one language and a common speech. As men moved eastward, they found a plain in Shinar and settled there. ... Then they said, "Come, let us build ourselves a city, with a tower that reaches to the heavens, so that we may make a name for ourselves and not be scattered over the face of the whole earth."
>
> *Genesis 11:1–4*

These people set out to make a name for themselves, without any regard for the love and faithfulness God had shown to them. They went so far as to defy God's command to be fruitful and fill the earth, saying "[let us] make a name for ourselves and *not* be scattered over the face of the whole earth." However, the Lord intervened. He came down to see the city and the tower the men were building. The Lord said:

> "If as one people speaking the same language they have begun to do this, then nothing they plan to do will be impossible for them. Come, let Us go down and confuse their language so they will not understand each other." So the Lord scattered them from there over all the earth, and they stopped building the city.
>
> *Genesis 11:6–8*

When we are tempted to make a name for ourselves at the expense of God's glory, or someone else's, we can remember the story of Babel. The arrogance behind that tower project was so disturbing to God that His division of the builders into different languages and different parts of the world still divides the human race today. Only God can bring lasting peace and unity to the world. This peace comes to us through the sacrifice of our Lord Jesus Christ. God's Son came as a humble servant, giving glory to His heavenly Father. Jesus humbled Himself to take our place on the cross. As the risen Christ, God has exalted Him to the place of highest honor and glory, victorious because of His unselfish love toward us.

As children of God through faith in Jesus, we pray "holy be Your name" by the power of the Holy Spirit. We reflect God's "good name" by taking our families to worship, praying with them, and spending time each day in family devotions. By God's grace, our families are blessed to walk humbly before God.

Dear Heavenly Father

When I feel the urge to take the credit others deserve or to keep the glory for success all to myself, remind me that I would have nothing without You. Make giving You glory for the good done in my life my greatest pleasure. In Jesus' name. Amen.

Today's Challenge

Starting today, avoid using the word *luck,* and conscientiously try to say "Lord willing" when telling others your plans, no matter how small those plans may be.

Read Psalm 53
Acts 2:1–13

WHEN GOD MAKES HIS NAME, EVERYTHING IS CLEAR

One of my colleagues in the ministry used to fly the C-130 Hercules transport plane in the United States Air Force. Being a bit of an aviation nut, I tried to steer this humble man into conversations that would uncover what it was like behind the controls of this mammoth aircraft.

One of my favorite stories has to do with a training video of a test flight. In this video, my colleague witnessed a C-130 attempting to land on an aircraft carrier. Dennis explained that the pilot basically would shut down the engines when the aircraft was over the carrier's flight deck, counting on the weight of the heavy C-130 to drop the aircraft onto the ship's deck like a rock.

Only one thing made the landing dangerous. You were not supposed to bring the throttle into the reverse engine position while in flight, as some of the engine props might push the plane backward while others continued to pull the plane forward. The confused directions of the four engines would cause the plane to crash instantly. It was essential that all four engines functioned together so the plane would fly straight. (Needless to say, the only piloting I will ever do is from my PC joystick.)

This C-130 information leads us to today's passage from the book of Acts:

Suddenly a sound like the blowing of a violent wind

came from heaven and filled the whole house where [the disciples] were sitting. They saw what seemed to be tongues of fire that separated and came to rest on each of them. All of them were filled with the Holy Spirit and began to speak in other tongues as the Spirit enabled them.

Acts 2:2–4

In our last devotion, we saw how God confused the language of arrogant men into all the languages that make up the human race today. This language confusion caused the tower of Babel project to crash. As a result, people were forced to spread out across the world just as God had commanded.

God always has a very good reason for everything He does. This confusion of languages kept humans' sinful pride in check. It would take God, not humans, to straighten out sin and its confusion in His own way and time. So God sent His Son, Jesus, to redeem us from our sins.

After Jesus died for all sin, rose again, and returned to heaven, God sent His Holy Spirit on Pentecost. The Jews had gathered in Jerusalem to celebrate the harvest. And what a harvest God had in store! By pouring Himself out unmistakably on Jesus' disciples through a sound like rushing wind and tongues of fire, the Holy Spirit made the name of Jesus clear for the first time to each nation in their own language. As the Gospel continues to be proclaimed today, the Holy Spirit enables us to believe that everything Jesus taught and did during His life on earth for our salvation is absolutely true!

We trust in God to graciously pilot our families through the confusing messages of our sinful society. By not distancing ourselves from the Word of God, the Holy Spirit does His work in our hearts. He strengthens our faith in Jesus, assures us that our sins are forgiven (even when we crash and burn), and gives us the peace that comes from knowing that for Jesus' sake God is no longer angry at us! The Holy Spirit blesses us with the joy that makes a name for God in our lives.

Heavenly Father

Give me an extra measure of Your Holy Spirit so I will always trust Jesus as my only Savior. Help me lead my family to You through Your Word. In Jesus' name. Amen.

Today's Challenge

If you do not do so already, take five or ten minutes each day for devotions with your family. Try to hold these devotions at the same time each day.

His Name Means Our Salvation

As a seminarian, I was looking up a word in a German dictionary. For fun, I decided to look up the word *pfaffe* as well. I was surprised to see that my last name meant "pastor" in German. Because I was studying to be a pastor, I thought that was pretty cool. I continued to think it was cool until one of my professors pointed out that *pfaffe* was more of a slang word, akin to calling a pastor a "preacher." Instead of proving that I was divinely chosen to lead a congregation, my name simply suggested that I was born to tell others what to do.

God graciously humbled me through this revelation. In various other ways, He humbles all of us so we do not think more of ourselves than we ought.

Speaking of names, God attaches great importance to the meaning of His name. If you and I want our names to be respected, how much more does God want His name to be honored and kept holy in our lives?

If you have not already done so, read Matthew 1:18–25. In this passage, an angel appeared to Joseph, the earthly father of Jesus, telling him that his soon-to-be wife, Mary, was going to give birth to a special baby. Pay attention to the significance of the name God gave to His Son:

> An angel of the Lord appeared to him in a dream and said, "Joseph son of David, do not be afraid to take Mary home as your wife, because what is conceived in her is from the Holy Spirit. She will give birth to a Son, and

you are to give Him the name Jesus, because He will save His people from their sins."

Matthew 1:20–21

In the gospel according to Luke, we see what Mary and Joseph did after Jesus was born: "On the eighth day, when it was time to circumcise Him, He was named Jesus, the name the angel had given Him before He had been conceived" (Luke 2:21).

Jesus has a name unlike any other. Although many people throughout history have been given the same name, no one other than Jesus of Nazareth was ever able to fulfill the meaning of the name *Jesus*. The name *Jesus* means "Yahweh (the Lord) saves" (Matthew 1:21). Every time Jesus' name is spoken, the speaker and listeners are reminded that God rescued humankind from sin, death, and hell through Jesus' precious blood.

Jesus is your Savior. From the time of His conception by the Holy Spirit, Jesus perfectly obeyed God's Law for you. This perfect obedience included both the ceremonial law governing Old Testament worship (circumcision and sacrifices), as well as the moral law (the Ten Commandments). Jesus fulfilled *everything* the Old Testament Scriptures said concerning the coming Savior by voluntarily going to the cross to be punished for all our sins. This was God's wonderful plan of love for you and me, the only way we could be permanently rescued from sin, death, and the power of the devil.

On the Last Day, when Jesus comes back to earth, He will give us a brand-new, perfect body. Then all believers will join together, praising our gracious Savior in heaven. St. Paul wrote in Philippians, "At the name of Jesus every knee should bow, in heaven and on earth and under the earth, and every tongue confess that Jesus Christ is Lord, to the glory of God the Father" (Philippians 2:10–11).

Saved through faith in Jesus alone, may we gladly devote our lives to bringing honor and praise to His glorious name! We honor Jesus by refusing to drag His name though the gutter and by frequently calling on Him with prayer, praise, and thanksgiving. In this way, people around us, beginning with our family members, will grow to know Jesus better as they see God's qualities of forgiveness, love, and compassion radiating from us. God enables us to live this way because Jesus' name means our salvation.

Dearest Jesus

Great is Your name above all names! In You alone do I put my trust. Forgive me when I misuse Your name. Help me, by the power of Your Holy Spirit, to use Your name to bring You only honor and glory. Enable me to lead my family into Your loving arms. In Your name. Amen.

Today's Challenge

If "Jesus Christ" is an expression you use for speech that does not praise God, stop using it this way. Use Jesus' name in ways that show others how important He is in your life.

Read Psalm 146
Matthew 2:1–12

Faith Must Drive Knowledge

When I was a kid, our family owned a cabin on a beautiful lake in central Minnesota. Every weekend during the summer, we went through the ritual of loading the boat with food, suitcases, beverages, fishing rods, tackle boxes, and my prized collection of G.I. Joes. Three generations of our family piled into the '72 Pontiac LeMans station wagon, and we were on our way "up north."

Imagine seven passengers ranging in age from 9 to 69! We still laugh about the time grandpa's tackle box fell off the roof and bounced down the road, exploding on the last bounce. My father was in the middle of stopping the car when grandpa already had the door open and one foot out. Not until I became the father of four children did I appreciate what that three-hour drive must have been like for my dad.

Such road trips, no matter how laborious, are nothing compared to the amazing road trip taken by the Wise Men, or *Magi*. Matthew records the story:

> After Jesus was born in Bethlehem in Judea, during the time of King Herod, Magi from the east came to Jerusalem and asked, "Where is the One who has been born King of the Jews? We saw His star in the east and have come to worship Him."
>
> *Matthew 2:1–2*

Matthew records for us the visit of the Magi. Although the popular song calls them "kings" and says there were

22

three, the Bible does not say how many came to visit the young child Jesus. The word *magi* suggests these visitors had a scholarly background, as opposed to the royal and wealthy background of kings.

Their point of origin is identified only as "the east." Many scholars have suggested a strong likelihood that these Magi came from the region near the Persian Gulf that was once ancient Babylon. Israel had spent several decades in Babylon as captive exiles because of their unfaithfulness to the Lord. While in Babylon, the Israelites probably witnessed their faith to their captors. It is likely that the Magi combined their knowledge of astronomy with what they read in the Hebrew Bible about the King of the Jews and were able to identify the Christmas star. Perhaps they had even read Numbers 24:17, 19a, which says, "A star will come out of Jacob; a scepter will rise out of Israel . . . a Ruler will come out of Jacob."

As we consider the great effort and personal expense these Magi made to travel as far as 900 miles, we stand in awe of their quest. From the Wise Men, we learn the value of knowledge and education. More important, we learn that faith (or trust) in God ought to drive knowledge instead of knowledge driving faith. As Jesus says in Mark 10:15, "I tell you the truth, anyone who will not receive the kingdom of God like a little child will never enter it."

As the Wise Men sought the promised King, God led them by the star, just as He leads us through the proclamation of the Good News of Him who died and rose again to save us from our sin. Through faith, our trips through life are blessed by our gracious and loving Savior. With outstretched arms, God welcomes His children to their heavenly final destination.

Heavenly Father

You led the Wise Men to Your Son, Jesus, by that special star and filled them with joy as they worshiped Him. Fill us with joy as we seek You in Your Holy Word. Keep us humble before You in childlike faith so our intellect might serve You rather than drive our faith. In Jesus' name. Amen.

Today's Challenge

Ask your children to draw small pictures of the Wise Men and the star they followed. Place these pictures in your car. Let the pictures remind you and your family that you travel through life by faith in Christ.

Read Psalm 112
James 4:1–3

God Helps Those Who Ask in Faith

"Cleanliness is next to godliness." "A good deed never goes unreturned." "God helps those who help themselves." What do these statements have in common? They are familiar sayings. They are also sayings that have elements of truth but are not true in and of themselves. For example, not everyone who has taken a bath is godly; many good deeds never get paid back; and God doesn't help only those who help themselves.

It is indeed true that God helps everyone, but the saying "God helps those who help themselves" is misleading. God's help is not based upon the condition that people first must help themselves. To show us the great love God has for all those who believe in His Son, Jesus Christ, it is as if God puts a blank check in our hands. Jesus said "Ask and it will be given to you; seek and you will find; knock and the door will be opened to you. For everyone who asks receives; he who seeks finds; and to him who knocks, the door will be opened" (Matthew 7:7–8). Are God's answers to prayers conditional? No. The Holy Spirit creates holy desires within the hearts of all who trust Jesus Christ alone for their salvation. These holy desires find expression in the things we ask of God in prayer. We can be assured that God will answer every prayer and provide His abiding strength and renewal.

The next thing Jesus says strikes home with parents, particularly dads:

> Which of you, if his son asks for bread, will give him a stone? Or if he asks for a fish, will give him a snake? If you, then, though you are evil, know how to give good gifts to your children, how much more will your Father in heaven give good gifts to those who ask Him!
>
> *Matthew 7:9–11*

Use whatever illustration you wish—gas money, bus fare, a fishing trip—they are all the same. If fathers, out of love, will do whatever they can to meet their children's needs and make them happy, and fathers are sinful human beings, how much more will our perfect heavenly Father bless His children with gifts that will last for all eternity?

What are these eternal gifts? In our Baptism, God the Holy Spirit created faith in our hearts. This faith is in Christ who died on the cross for our salvation. God continues to exercise this faith, drawing us closer to Him through Word and sacraments in worship and in daily devotions with our families. As our faith in Jesus grows, the Holy Spirit helps us express this faith in a lifestyle pleasing to God.

Dads, if someone handed you a blank check, only the wise would appreciate its true worth. Such an individual would think carefully about how he would maximize its value. He would endeavor to use it for the greatest good. In the same way, you, a child of God, are called to use the blank check of prayer God has given to you. Ask for that which will eternally benefit you, your wife, and your children spiritually—forgiveness of sins, stronger faith, and strength to fight temptation. As you make other requests, pray that God's will be done for the sake of His Son and your Savior, Jesus Christ. Through faith in Jesus, know that God always will help you and those entrusted to your care.

Dear Heavenly Father

Thank You for Your promise to answer my prayers in ways that are best for me. Guide me to ask for what is pleasing to You, that I and my family may grow strong in our faith by the power of Your Holy Spirit. In Jesus' name. Amen.

Today's Challenge

Jot down what you typically ask of God. If the list is mostly "daily bread" items (things for this earthly life), add spiritual items (forgiveness, increased humility, courage to tell others about Jesus, etc.). Include prayers for the needs of other people, and remember to give special thanks to God for the blessings in your life.

Read Psalm 22
Matthew 27:27–56

Thank God Jesus Did Not Save Himself

C.Y.O.R. Do you know what these initials stand for? They stand for "Cover Your Own Rear"! Whether you are white collar, blue-collar, or (like me) plastic-collar, it is human nature to protect ourselves from harm. Perhaps the best way to protect ourselves is by avoiding harmful situations altogether.

Where would you and I be if God believed in the C.Y.O.R. philosophy? What if Jesus would have avoided the agonizing pain of the cross instead of suffering and dying for our sins? For one thing, you would not be reading this book because there would be no Good News to share. Thankfully, you are reading this book. Because of Jesus' unconditional love, there is a whole world of Good News to proclaim!

In Matthew, we witness Jesus' answer to the C.Y.O.R. crowd:

> Then the governor's soldiers took Jesus into the Praetorium and gathered the whole company of soldiers around Him. They stripped Him and put a scarlet robe on Him, and then twisted together a crown of thorns and set it on His head. They put a staff in His right hand and knelt in front of Him and mocked Him. "Hail, king of the Jews!" they said. They spit on Him, and took the staff and struck Him on the head again and again. After they had mocked Him, they took off the robe and put His own clothes on Him. Then they led Him away to crucify Him.

Matthew 27:27–31

Our Lord could have ended His agony anytime He wanted. An early departure, however, would have left us hopeless in eternal despair. God made known His commitment to the human race when He first promised Adam and Eve that He would send a Savior (Genesis 3:15). This salvation, however, would cost God the suffering and death of His own Son! As you read the entire lesson from Matthew 27:27–56, consider how Jesus put you and your family's needs ahead of His own as He hung in agony on that cursed tree.

Instead of saving Himself, as His tormentors dared Him to do, Jesus stayed on the cross. On that awful altar, the one perfect offering for the punishment, guilt, and curse of all sin was made. Jesus did not save Himself because He came to this earth to save all of us.

The Good News doesn't end on the cross. Three days later God raised His Son from the dead. In the resurrection of Jesus, we have God's personal promise that those who believe in His Son for their salvation will be raised with perfect, sinless bodies on the Last Day. All of our loved ones who believe in Jesus will be raised along with every believer since Adam and Eve. What a happy family reunion that Day will be!

As you sit here, you know how the Lord wants you to handle potential harm in your life. First, trust God. He alone is worthy of all your faith. Second, pray often, knowing that He hears you and answers your prayers according to His perfect will. Third, with His help, put the needs of others—beginning with your wife and children—ahead of your own. Look at each potentially harmful situation as an opportunity to give honor and glory to God by handling it in a God-pleasing way. You will be amazed how often the situations are not as bad as you thought. Finally, thank

God! For whether you live or die, you have the reassurance of eternal life with Jesus.

Dear Lord Jesus

By not saving Yourself from Your enemies, You saved me from mine: sin, death, and the power of the devil. Thank You. I ask that You give me strength to live my life unselfishly to Your honor and glory. In Your holy name. Amen.

Today's Challenge

Identify one thing you are afraid of right now. Pray for wisdom and guidance that you may choose a God-pleasing course of action. Leave the situation in the Lord's hands and trust in His all-knowing ways.

Read Psalm 8
1 Peter 1:8–9
John 20:19–31

Not Seeing Is Believing

Often we hear the expression "Seeing is believing." God tells us that with Him the opposite is true. If there is one point made clear in God's Word, it is that He wants us to trust Him. Period. Quite simply, God is not obligated to prove His existence to us any more than a potter is obligated to prove his existence to the lump of clay on his wheel. Anything God does for you and me is done purely out of His mercy and undeserved love. The question is "Who is the clay, and Who is the Potter?"

God makes Himself known to us because He loves us. St. John wrote:

> Then [Jesus] said to Thomas, "Put your finger here; see My hands. Reach out your hand and put it into My side. Stop doubting and believe." Thomas said to Him, "My Lord and my God!" Then Jesus told him, "Because you have seen Me, you have believed; blessed are those who have not seen and yet have believed." Jesus did many other miraculous signs in the presence of His disciples, which are not recorded in this book. But these are written that you may believe that Jesus is the Christ, the Son of God, and that by believing you may have life in His name.
>
> *John 20:27–31*

We can love God because He first loved us! After all, He sent His Son, Jesus, to earth who, by His perfect life and His innocent suffering and death on the cross, delivered us all from eternal damnation. Trust Him without physically seeing Him. Trust Him on the basis of His Word alone, which never fails us.

There were an abundance of eyewitnesses who saw everything you hear and read in Holy Scripture. The apostle John witnessed both Thomas's doubt and Thomas's joy in seeing the Lord. John testified, "That which was from the beginning, which we have heard, which we have seen with our eyes, which we have looked at and our hands have touched—this we proclaim concerning the Word of life" (1 John 1:1).

Through His Word, God strengthens our faith in Jesus Christ. On account of our trust in the crucified and risen Savior, we faithfully interpret every word and event recorded in the Bible as for our salvation. As you read the Bible with your family, tell your children that everything written in the Bible is God's Word. Tell your children that Jesus is talking to *them* when He says, "Blessed are those who have not seen and yet have believed."

Gracious Father

Thank You for loving me the way You do. Although I cannot see You physically with my eyes, I can trust You through the eyes of faith. Help me lead my family to hear You each day through Your Word until the Day we all see You face-to-face in heaven. In Jesus' precious name. Amen.

Today's Challenge

As you drive or walk today, think about all the things that exist in the "natural world" although you cannot see them (e.g.: atoms, radio waves, the layers of molten rock beneath the earth's crust). Give thanks to God that you know the Creator of this awesome world. Give thanks that you know how much He loves you in Jesus.

—————

Only the Genuine Article Will Save You

We live in an age of *knockoffs*. It is not difficult to purchase a Rolex watch on the streets of New York for $25 or "genuine 18K gold jewelry" that is 10K at best. To separate their products from the fakes and cheap imitations, the Levi Strauss Company proudly displays the slogan "The Genuine Article" on their rather large tags. In an age where "buyer beware" is necessary consumer wisdom, we feel fortunate when we find a quality piece of merchandise.

St. Paul was passionately concerned that the teachings about Jesus Christ be accepted as "quality." So the believers might know the authenticity of his testimony, he wrote:

> I want you to know, brothers, that the gospel I preached is not something man made up. I did not receive it from any man, nor was I taught it; rather I received it by revelation from Jesus Christ.
>
> *Galatians 1:11–12*

In his first letter to the Corinthians, Paul proclaimed Christ Jesus crucified, buried, and risen to save us all from our sins according to the Scriptures. To assure his readers that these were not inflated claims about Jesus of Nazareth, Paul wrote:

> [Jesus] appeared to Peter, and then to the Twelve. After that, He appeared to more than five hundred of the

brothers at the same time, most of whom are still living, though some have fallen asleep.

1 Corinthians 15:5–6

The next time you meet someone who does not believe that Jesus Christ rose from the dead, ask them this: How many witnesses does it take to prove in a court of law that something happened? It takes two witnesses whose stories agree. Additional witnesses cement the case.

By citing eyewitness testimony, the apostle Paul leads his readers to the certainty that Jesus truly is the Savior of the world. Yet it is only by the power of the Holy Spirit that any of us can call Jesus Lord and Savior. Through the means of grace—the Word of God, Holy Baptism, and the Lord's Supper—the Holy Spirit creates saving faith in our hearts. By those same means, He strengthens and sustains our faith in Jesus as our only Savior from sin.

As we lead our families faithfully to God's Word and sacraments, the Holy Spirit cements the certainty that Jesus Christ is "The Genuine Article" who saves us.

Dear Lord Jesus

Forgive me when I am tempted to not see You as the source for help in my life. You alone are my Savior and my Helper at all times. Let me never be led away from You by false teaching, but keep me and my family faithful to You. In Your holy name. Amen.

Today's Challenge

Knowing how important it is to discern false teaching, set aside time in your daily schedule for individual Bible study or Bible study with friends or coworkers. Ask your pastor for guidance or suggestions.

A Costly Cover-up

The word *cover-up* is familiar in recent American history. Conspiracy theories abound regarding the assassinations of John F. Kennedy and Dr. Martin Luther King Jr., Watergate, the Iran-Contra Affair, and the escapades of William Jefferson Clinton. Americans have learned to look at almost any historic event with a jaundiced eye, reluctant to believe any claim of fact.

As we turn to the gospel account of St. Matthew, we find that conspiracies to cover up the truth are not new. Although the soldiers guarding Jesus' tomb felt the earthquake and saw an angel of the Lord roll the stone away from the entrance of the tomb, the Good News of Jesus' resurrection was covered up. Matthew wrote:

> Some of the guards went into the city and reported to the chief priests everything that had happened. When the chief priests had met with the elders and devised a plan, they gave the soldiers a large sum of money, telling them, "You are to say, 'His disciples came during the night and stole Him away while we were asleep.' If this report gets to the governor, we will satisfy him and keep you out of trouble." So the soldiers took the money and did as they were instructed. And this story has been widely circulated among the Jews to this very day.
>
> *Matthew 28:11–15*

So incredibly hard are the hearts of wicked and unbelieving! If you were one of those guards and the angel of God had just terrified you at Jesus' tomb, wouldn't you want to do everything in your power not to anger God? Wouldn't you laugh at the thought of taking money in exchange for lying about the all-powerful God you just discovered existed?

The conspiracy and collusion of enemies, born of hatred and unbelief, could not sweep the truth of Jesus' resurrection under the rug. To proclaim the Good News that Jesus died on the cross for our sins and rose again from the dead, God made very average men, women, and children His personal spokespersons. God turned the uninfluential, the weak, the poor, and those without much education (or none at all) into the bearers of the only news that saves humankind from the eternal despair of hell. Those who conceived and carried out the conspiracy to cover up the truth of Jesus' resurrection are long since dead. The glorious truth of Jesus' death and resurrection, however, is still boldly proclaimed.

Satan still works hard to cover up the news that Jesus is alive. Those who believe Satan's conspiracy will pay with their souls. Like those first disciples who heard and spread the Good News of Jesus Christ, God has called us to the lifelong business of setting the record straight. Every time you take your family to worship to hear the truth of God's Word and commune at the Lord's Table, the Lord strengthens and preserves you against the devil's deceptions.

Heavenly Father

You went to such great lengths to secure our salvation through the suffering, death, and resurrection of Your beloved Son, Jesus. Let no one deceive us into doubting the truth of our Savior's resurrection. And let no one deceive us into doubting the truth of our own resurrection through Jesus. In His precious name. Amen.

Today's Challenge

Think of all the things for which people are willing to jeopardize their soul: sexual pleasure, money, a promotion, etc. Compare those things the world considers important with the price Jesus paid on the cross for the forgiveness of your sins. Because of Jesus' death and resurrection, your soul is safe with Him and you can enjoy your earthly life under His gracious care.

Head Knowledge or Heart Knowledge?

Are you good at memory work, or does that question send shivers up your spine? As a pastor, I have seen students employ a variety of techniques to satisfy their memory work requirement.

First, there is the "hydraulic" method. In this method, the student waits until the very last minute before class to start memorizing, then forces the required memory work into the brain with the same relentless force of a hydraulic pump.

Second, there is the ever popular "I'm not very good at memorizing" method. In this method, the student combines the art of persuasion with a stall technique, hoping the pastor will either give him or her a pass, or ignore the requirement out of fatigue.

The final approach to memory work is what I like to call the "right" method. The "right" method does not force material into the brain. Rather, the material is read aloud repeatedly over several days. The student slowly digests the material instead of being force-fed. My confirmation students are used to hearing Pastor Pfaffe say, "I do not want this [memory work] in your head, but in your heart!"

This little lesson in memorization techniques demonstrates a principle regarding faith that is expressed through

God's Word. Is it enough to believe certain events recorded in the Bible actually happened, or is something besides head knowledge involved? To answer this question, turn to today's lesson from Acts chapter seven.

St. Stephen had been brought before the Jewish ruling council (the Sanhedrin) by men who were trying to stop him from preaching Jesus Christ as Savior. These religious leaders were filled with head knowledge—the facts, dates, and events of the Bible. They did not, however, have heart knowledge. Look at what happened after Stephen used Scripture to prove that Jesus was God's long awaited Messiah (God's Anointed One):

> When [the Sanhedrin] heard this, they were furious and gnashed their teeth at him. But Stephen, full of the Holy Spirit, looked up to heaven and saw the glory of God, and Jesus standing at the right hand of God. "Look," he said, "I see heaven open and the Son of Man standing at the right hand of God." At this they covered their ears and, yelling at the top of their voices, they all rushed at him, dragged him out of the city and began to stone him.
>
> *Acts 7:54–58*

Imagine! This was an elite group of highly dignified men, proud of their knowledge of the Scriptures, proud of their social standing, and proud of the respect they commanded within Israel. Yet because of Stephen's witness for Jesus, these proud and dignified men completely unraveled. They went so far as to condemn Stephen to death. It wasn't Stephen's personality nor his personal ambitions that were a threat to the Sanhedrin. The sheer power of God's Word proclaimed by Stephen drove these men into the rage that resulted in his martyrdom. Stephen had heart knowledge. He had faith that trusted in Jesus as his only Savior from sin. All the head knowledge of Scripture would not have done the Sanhedrin any good if it wasn't believed in their hearts.

As learning more of God's Word becomes a priority in life, remember that this is not merely an intellectual pursuit. It is with the heart that we believe Jesus died on the cross to take away our sins. Within our hearts, we believe that He rose again to guarantee our own resurrection to eternal life on the Last Day. Thank God that His Holy Spirit, who came into our hearts through our Baptism, continues to strengthen our faith. Built up and strengthened by God's Word and sacraments, we never need to fear that our head knowledge lacks the most important heart knowledge—saving faith!

Dear Jesus

Thank You for the gift of Your saving love. Through the power of the Holy Spirit, grant me the knowledge that trusts in You alone for salvation. In Your name. Amen.

Today's Challenge

Try to remember every meal eaten this week and last. Can you do it? Even if you can't, ask yourself, "Did I eat? Am I well fed now?" In the same way, God feeds us with His Word and sacraments, although our minds cannot understand or remember everything He has fed to us. Thank the Lord for His work in our lives.

God's 180

Have you ever wondered what it takes to make a large passenger jet stop rolling down the runway? I once asked an airline pilot this very question. He said there are several braking systems on a large aircraft working in concert to bring the plane from approximately 130 miles per hour to a smooth stop. One is the system of spoilers on the wings that create a drag of wind resistance. Another is the system of wheel brakes. Perhaps most interesting is the braking system of the reverse-thrust engines. As the aircraft lands, the pilot throws the engines into reverse. This sends the thrust out the front, pushing the aircraft backward, and slowing the plane dramatically.

What does this tidbit of aviation information have to do with today's Scripture reading from Acts? The answer is this: With God as the Pilot in our lives, the Holy Spirit works as our reverse thrust engines, turning us 180 degrees.

God has always been in the business of redirecting people's lives 180 degrees. He reversed the course of humankind from a deadly collision with eternal death in hell, back to eternal life with Him in heaven. One of the greatest examples of God's power is seen in the life of St. Paul. You may recall that St. Paul originally went by the name of Saul from the city of Tarsus.

As a young man, Saul thought the biggest favor he could do for God was to exterminate the Christian religion. He even held the coats of those who stoned St. Stephen, the first Christian martyr (Acts 7:59–8:1).

One day, while Saul was traveling to the city of Damascus to persecute Christians, Jesus appeared to him in a blinding light, asking why he was persecuting Him. What could Saul say but "Who are You, Lord?" (Acts 9:5).

Jesus wasted no time throwing on major braking systems in Saul's life, blinding him and commanding him to go into the city where he would be told what to do (Acts 9:6).

In a vision, the Lord called to a disciple named Ananias and told him to place his hands on Saul. God used Ananias to restore Saul's sight and to baptize him. Read what happened to show the awesome power of God to change the direction in people's lives from eternal death to eternal life with Him:

> At once [Saul/Paul] began to preach in the synagogues that Jesus is the Son of God. All those who heard him were astonished and asked, "Isn't he the man who raised havoc in Jerusalem among those who call on this name? And hasn't he come here to take them as prisoners to the chief priests?" Yet Saul grew more and more powerful and baffled the Jews living in Damascus by proving that Jesus is the Christ.
>
> *Acts 9:20–22*

Clearly God is the Pilot, the Initiator who begins and completes our salvation. God sent His only Son to obey the Ten Commandments in our place, and to be punished for our sins. Saul learned that all along Jesus' death on the cross had been the most important part of God's plan to save the world!

Jesus absorbed the anger of God that we deserved so we could be declared not guilty forever for Jesus' sake. God put the reverse engines into gear when Jesus died and rose again. His Holy Spirit works through water and His Word to create a faith in our hearts that trusts in Jesus alone for full forgiveness. God continues to nourish our faith as we listen to His Word and receive the Lord's Supper faithfully, and trust in His promise to forgive our sins in Jesus' name.

We can no more turn the direction of our lives from death to life than an airplane can decide to reverse itself. Trusting that God has chosen us to be His own provides all the encouragement husbands and fathers need to make sure their families know Jesus through a faithful and consistent worship life in family devotions, daily prayers, and Sunday worship.

Dear Jesus

Help me by the power of Your Holy Spirit to never forget that You alone rescued me from certain, eternal death. Thank You! In Your name. Amen.

Today's Challenge

Look at the size of the airplanes and jets that fly over head every day. Remember that God's power is much greater than that of their engines!

Read Psalm 111
1 Corinthians 2:6–16

God's Secret Wisdom

One of my early memories as a kid in the '60s was Sunday evenings—frozen pizza on TV trays and *Mission Impossible* on TV. I may not remember the details of any single episode, but every week I looked forward to seeing that tape smoking in the tape player. Looking back, it's easy to understand why that tape had to smoke. That "impossible" mission had to be kept secret.

A wise man once said, "Everything we say needs to be the truth, but then again, not all truth needs to be said." Some information is best kept private between only those individuals whom it concerns. God has information of His own that the Bible calls wisdom. God's wisdom is mysterious as it belongs only to those who trust in His Son, Jesus, for salvation from sin.

To help describe this secret wisdom of God, we turn to today's reading from St. Paul:

 We do, however, speak a message of wisdom among the mature, but not the wisdom of this age or of the rulers of this age, who are coming to nothing. No, we speak of God's secret wisdom, a wisdom that has been hidden and that God destined for our glory before time began. None of the rulers of this age understood it, for if they had, they would not have crucified the Lord of glory. However, as it is written: "No eye has seen, no ear has heard, no mind has conceived what God has prepared for those who love Him"—but God has revealed it to us by His Spirit.

1 Corinthians 2:6–10

If you have ever tried to tell someone at work about Jesus or have refused to join in making fun of someone, you have most likely discovered that those who do not trust Christ simply do not understand you. People who do not believe in Jesus regard worship as a bore, sin as fun, and heaven and hell as states of mind rather than real places. St. Paul states that there is a very good reason why you are so different from the unbelieving friend, co-worker, or even family member. What makes you different is your faith in God's wisdom, not the so-called wisdom of the world.

The world's "wisdom" is faith in one's self, while God's wisdom is faith in God. The world's "wisdom" is to elevate one's self, even at the expense of others. God's wisdom is to serve God, others, and then yourself. The world's "wisdom" then pursues whatever pleases the earthly body. God's wisdom understands that drawing from God's Word, Holy Baptism, and the Lord's Supper is as necessary as breathing. The world's "wisdom" fears death and clings to life at all costs. God's wisdom leads us to die to ourselves and live according to our love and trust in Jesus who conquered our death by His death on the cross for the forgiveness of all sins.

By the power of God's Holy Spirit working through our Baptism, we have come to confess that Jesus is the true God and true man who lived a perfect life as our substitute under God's Ten Commandments. By Jesus' suffering and death as our substitute, God's anger was paid for in full. Jesus' resurrection from the dead is our personal guarantee that we too will rise again on the Last Day.

The wisdom God reveals to us in faith ought not be kept a secret any longer. God is eager for us to share this secret until the whole world knows Jesus as their Savior and Lord. On that great day, when Jesus returns in glory, we will experience what "No eye has seen, no ear has heard." Indeed "no mind has conceived what God has prepared for those who love Him."

Dear Jesus

Allow my words and actions to reflect Your gracious love so the secret of Your wisdom might be shared with everyone I meet! In Your name. Amen.

Today's Challenge

Consider the statements that pass for "wisdom" in the world today (i.e., statements made by intellectual elites, movies acclaimed as profound and deep in meaning, attributes and objects deemed valuable and worth imitating). What impact do these have on attitude toward those who trust in Jesus alone for salvation?

Read Psalm 34
1 Corinthians 6:12–20

Real Men Run Away

The 1990s were known for many things: the Internet, rap music, the "Don't ask—Don't tell" policy, and the return of the Volkswagen Beetle, to name a few. The 1990s were also known as the decade of the sensitive male. Society has tried very hard to redefine the "real" man. In the past, "real" men did not cry; now they do. "Real" men used to provide for their families; today the presence of a father figure in the home is often not considered as necessary as was once believed. In the old days, a "real" man was someone like John Wayne or Gary Cooper; today a real man is someone like Montel Williams or Jerry Springer.

In response to this great identity crisis, these words from St. Paul provide one criteria that defines what a real man is, or rather, what a real man does, from God's point of view:

> Flee from sexual immorality. All other sins a man commits are outside his body, but he who sins sexually sins against his own body. Do you not know that your body is a temple of the Holy Spirit, who is in you, whom you have received from God? You are not your own; you were bought at a price. Therefore honor God with your body.
>
> *1 Corinthians 6:18–20*

According to Paul, a real man of God runs away where sin is concerned. For example, sexuality can be a particularly weak spot in the makeup of men. Society encourages men to loosen up (as if we needed any help!). God, though, consistently teaches us in His Word to "Watch out!" and "Beware!" of sexual sin. But why? If it feels good, why not do it? What harm is done?

You do not have to be a Christian to know that cheating on your spouse is foolish and destructive. The pain of sexual promiscuity has ripped apart many families. The rise in school violence and rage of our youth has increased along with the rising number of broken families. There seems to be an absence of husbands and fathers and an overabundance of boyfriends and live-in companions. There appears to be a tendency of self-absorption among adults at the expense of their children.

Yet the underlying cause for these destructive behaviors is always the same—sin. And the damage of sin has eternal consequences.

What is God's answer to the sad reality of sin? You read it earlier: "You are not your own; you were bought at a price." Contrary to protest signs in pro-abortion rallies that read "Our Bodies—Our Choice," the truth is that none of us—male or female, Christian or non-Christian— owns our body. The whole world has been bought at a price, and that price is the precious blood of God's Son, our Lord Jesus Christ.

Death and separation from God became reality when Adam and Eve sinned. Out of His great love for the whole human race, God chose to redeem us, to buy us back at great personal cost. For everyone who trusts in Jesus, by the power of the Holy Spirit working through God's Word and sacraments, God guarantees eternal life.

Society will continue to try to define a "real" man. We, however, trust that God sent His Son, Jesus, as the Real Man to live the perfect life in our place. He met sin head-on and suffered our punishment on the cross to buy us back for Himself. We can show our gratitude for this eternal love by striving to be "real men of God," grasping the strength that is ours through Jesus, looking sin in the eye, then turning away.

Dear Jesus

Thank You for the victory over sin that is mine through Your life, death, and resurrection. Help me to always run to You, and turn away from selfish behavior that only gratifies my own needs. In Your name. Amen.

Today's Challenge

Consider all the examples of "real" men on television, in movies, and in advertisements. What connections, if at all, exist between these portrayals and sin as evidenced in the media?

BE THE BEST BODY PART YOU CAN BE

"Be all that you can be." Quick! Who coined that phrase? That's right, the United States Army. The phrase is taken from a recruitment commercial. The armed forces have used catchy tunes and motivating themes to their advantage. They promise to make their recruits the best they can be for the duration of their enlistment.

God also desires His children to perform at their best. An important difference between soldiers in the Lord's Army and those in the United States Army is that the tour of duty in the Lord's Army is lifelong and beyond! St. Paul expressed it this way:

> The body is a unit, though it is made up of many parts; and though all its parts are many, they form one body. So it is with Christ. For we were all baptized by one Spirit into one body—whether Jews or Greeks, slave or free—and we were all given the one Spirit to drink. ... Now you are the body of Christ, and each one of you is a part of it.
>
> *1 Corinthians 12:12, 27*

As you read the whole lesson selected for today, ask yourself this question: *What gifts or talents has God given to me?* To discover the answers, you might ask, *What is my career? Do I like to work with my hands? Do I like to sing, play a musical instrument, cook? Can I work well with numbers? Do I enjoy writing? Can I talk in front of large groups of people without fainting? Do I enjoy troubleshooting challenging problems? Do I like talking to young people, adults, or the elderly?*

We are all members of Christ's body, each with unique talents and abilities. All the diverse interests and personalities join together to form God's Church through our Baptism in Christ. Christians cannot opt out of Christ's body any more than a soldier can opt out of working with his or her fellow soldiers.

Personal reflection now and then helps us consider how God blesses us and moves us to gratitude in serving Him well. Merely taking such an inventory, however, would fall far short of the point in today's lesson. Paul's point is more than taking stock of what gifts and talents we have. He urges us to use those talents in ways that reflect God's care for our fellow body parts—our brothers and sisters in Christ.

Such use of our gifts and talents are the fruits of trusting that God sent His Son to die on the cross for the salvation of our sins. When we were baptized, God did something wonderful: He connected us to the body of Christ through Christ's blood poured out for us on the cross. Since no one can go back in time and steal away our Baptism, the daily washing away of our sins' guilt and punishment is guaranteed by Christ Himself. As baptized members of His body, we express the saving faith the Holy Spirit has created in our hearts through loving actions and words toward our brothers and sisters in Christ.

Men can thank God that He has given them a special privilege and responsibility as fathers and husbands. Not only is it their job to care for the physical bodies of their wives and children, but to care especially for their families as members of Christ's body. The greatest care a man can give his family is to create and foster an atmosphere within the home that clearly shows that Christ is the head of the household. The members of the family are His hands, feet, eyes, ears, and lips. Through weekly worship, home devotions, mealtime and bedtime prayers, and conversations about God's love in Christ, children will trust they belong to the body of Christ just as much as mom and dad.

When our tour of duty in the Lord's Army for this life is up, the retirement waiting for us in heaven beats any pension plan offered in this world!

Heavenly Father

Give me the strength, the wisdom, and the faithfulness to use the gifts and talents You have given me to make Christ's Body—His Church—stronger than it would be without me. In Jesus' name. Amen.

Today's Challenge

If you are part of a team at work or in another organization, consider how much more work gets done when everyone knows their job and does their best. The church, when faithful to its Head, Jesus Christ, is the same.

Read Psalm 16
1 Corinthians 15:12–20

Don't Believe in the Resurrection? Then Give It Up!

Life is _____. How would you finish this sentence? Would you fill the blank in with something positive like *wonderful, beautiful,* or *amazing*? Or, would you be more pessimistic? Unfortunately, many people today feel that life is negative and bleak. To them, living from day-to-day seems hopeless, pointless, and even agonizing. Some believe that death is merely the sad end to a sad life. For a person who does not believe in Christ's resurrection, life is bleak indeed. St. Paul wrote:

> But if it is preached that Christ has been raised from the dead, how can some of you say that there is no resurrection of the dead? ... If Christ has not been raised, our preaching is useless and so is your faith. ... And if Christ has not been raised, your faith is futile; you are still in your sins. ... If only for this life we have hope in Christ, we are to be pitied more than all men.
>
> *1 Corinthians 15:12–19*

Read the title for this devotion: "Don't Believe in the Resurrection? Then, Give It Up!" That's the point Paul is making here. The city of Corinth was, in ancient Greece, a major port on the Aegean Sea. For the church in that city, the apostle had to deal with two specific problems: immorality and rejection of the idea that dead people can come back to life.

Paul cut right to the chase. He, in essence, told the Corinthians, "If you don't believe that the dead can come back to life, then neither can Christ. If Christ has not come back from the dead, then He cannot be your Savior from sin. If He is not your Savior, then you are stuck with your sins and heaven is closed to you." What kind of good news is that for Christians?

Think of the hardship, animosity, and persecution our brothers and sisters in Christ have endured throughout the history of the world all for the name of our Savior Jesus Christ. The world hated Christ. Christ warned His disciples that the world would hate His followers too, because they would bear His name in their lives. If being a Christian was all about suffering on earth without the promise of resurrection in Jesus Christ, "loser" might be a more fitting title for each one of us.

Fortunately, 1 Corinthians confidently assures us that we are not losers, "But Christ has indeed been raised from the dead, the firstfruits of those who have fallen asleep" (1 Corinthians 15:20). The message is this, *Where Christ has gone, we will follow!* Because Jesus rose from the dead after conquering sin, death, and the power of the devil, we will follow when God raises us up with brand-new, perfectly glorified bodies on the day He returns.

Trusting that the resurrection is real provides us with many blessings today. We can be assured that our heavenly Father accepted His Son's sacrifice on the cross as payment in full for the guilt and punishment of our sins. We can rest in God's peace, knowing that He is no longer angry with us for Jesus' sake. This peace also springs from the knowledge that our lives and the lives of our wives and children are safe in His watchful eyes and protective arms. We can turn the other cheek, letting go of the nagging temptation to seek revenge when we have been treated unfairly. God has promised to settle all matters in this life in His own fair and just way on the Last Day.

By the power of the Holy Spirit working in our lives through Baptism, His Word, and the Lord's Supper, we can seize every opportunity to tell people about the truth of the resurrection. We can live in joyful anticipation of the resurrection and let its joy put grief in proper perspective.

O Holy Spirit

Protect me from doubts that rob me of the comfort I have knowing Jesus is risen from the dead. Give me confidence of my resurrection on the Last Day. In Jesus' name. Amen.

Today's Challenge

Next time you are channel surfing and come across a televangelist, see if the message of the resurrection comes across loud and clear. If the focus of the message is on anything other than the cross of Christ and His resurrection, ask yourself, "What purpose does this message serve?"

Read Psalm 23
1 Corinthians 15:35–49

Don't Like Your Body? Just Wait!

The other day, I decided it was time to go back on The Diet. I went into the pantry to retrieve the box of oatmeal used the last time I went on The Diet. As I poured my first bowl, I noticed two dead bugs in my oatmeal! I turned to my wife, Debbie, and said, "This oatmeal doesn't have much of a shelf life, does it?" That's when she reminded me that it had been almost a year since I had last put it away.

The two dead bugs reminded me that time passes more quickly than I realize. Before you know it, the living things around you have gotten old; some have decayed, and some have even died.

As natural as death and decay are for all things living, humans still try with all their might to keep death and decay from happening to them. The billions of dollars spent in America on health and beauty aids are proof of the never-ending effort to cheat old age and even death itself. Whether we care a whole lot about our looks or not at all, today's devotion speaks to all of us who will one day taste death. St. Paul wrote:

> But someone may ask, "How are the dead raised? With what kind of body will they come?" How foolish! What you sow does not come to life unless it dies. ... So will it be with the resurrection of the dead. The body that is sown is perishable, it is raised imperishable. ... And just as we have borne the likeness of the earthly man, so shall we bear the likeness of the Man from heaven.
>
> *1 Corinthians 15:35–49*

To describe the truth of Christ's resurrection from the dead, St. Paul used the sowing of seed as an example. The farmer plants a tiny seed of corn so a new ear of corn can grow. As this illustration explains the mystery how death is necessary in the process of rebirth, it also demonstrates God's wisdom in making death a necessary part of our life. Like the old seed of corn, our old bodies return to the earth. Hoping to have a body without sickness, deformity, and weariness from age, means trusting the body we now live in has to die.

For the person who does not believe in the resurrection, death poses a problem. However, for us who know Jesus as our Savior, the meaning of death has completely changed in our lives. Death now becomes God's servant. Instead of a dark hole into which humans fall at the end of their lives, Christ has made death a doorway through which we enter paradise. Death becomes a dressing room in which we take off our worn-out, sin-stained body and put on the robe of righteousness that was washed in the blood of our Lord Jesus Christ.

We enjoy these robes firsthand when we die, but the robes of righteousness are already ours! Christ purchased them for us through His perfect life, death, and resurrection. We were covered with His righteousness from the moment we were baptized, when the Holy Spirit gave us saving faith in our Lord Jesus Christ. On the great day when Christ returns, we will be changed and given a very real, spiritual body completely free of sin.

But what are we to do now? We are to use the body God has given us in service to Him and others. As husbands and fathers, God wants us to care for the bodies of our family members. Most important, however, God charges men with the awesome responsibility of nurturing their wives and children with the Word of God and the holy sacraments.

As your faith and your family's faith in Jesus continues to grow and mature, you can look forward to that great day when we will trade in these present bodies for the new bodies Christ will give us. If your present body gives you trouble now, just wait!

Lord Jesus

Remind us when we feel discouraged with our present bodies, that the day is coming when we shall rise again with new bodies and see You in glory. In Your name. Amen.

Today's Challenge

Take your children to a garden store and show them different kinds of bulbs. If you ask them if the bulbs look pretty, they will probably tell you they look ugly. Take one of the ugly bulbs home and plant it. When a beautiful flower comes up, tell your children that God will take our bodies, made ugly by sin, and raise them up beautiful and perfect when Jesus comes back on the Last Day!

This Kind of Change Is Good

What thoughts does the word *change* bring to mind? I'm not talking about pennies and nickels. I'm talking about the active state of change and transition. Do you like *change*, or do you do everything in your power to avoid it?

Some people think of change as new opportunities for excitement, adventure, and fun. After all, change might bring hopes of a promotion with better pay, a nicer work environment, or more challenging assignments.

But to others, change strikes terror in their hearts, presenting new situations that are both unfamiliar and frightening. They might ask, *What if this change takes away the comfort and security of our routine? If I won't be able to adapt to the change, will I be criticized?* But like everything in life, even change is what God makes of it.

In today's devotion, we conclude the "resurrection chapter" of 1 Corinthians 15. As we think about the beautiful promise God makes to us in these verses, we can all rest assured that our coming resurrection will be a good change. St. Paul wrote:

> I declare to you, brothers, that flesh and blood cannot inherit the kingdom of God, nor does the perishable inherit the imperishable. Listen, I tell you a mystery: We will not all sleep, but we will all be changed—in a flash, in the twinkling of an eye, at the last trumpet. For the trumpet will sound, the dead will be raised imperishable, and we will be changed.
>
> *1 Corinthians 15:50–52*

As a pastor, it amazes me how many people think we become angels when we go to heaven. When this topic of death and resurrection comes up, my response is, "Why would you want to settle for being an angel?" Of course there's nothing wrong with being an angel, but God has made human beings even more important than angels. The best proof of the special love and importance God has placed upon humans is seen when we compare God's respective responses to the angels and the human beings when sin entered the picture.

When Satan and all of the angels who followed him turned against God and rebelled, God prepared a prison for these evil angels called *hell*. These angels are living in hell right now, awaiting the final judgment. When Adam and Eve sinned, God immediately went into action on their behalf. He planned the salvation of the human race and sent His only begotten Son to our world to die on the cross for our sins. To accomplish this, Jesus changed from glory and life to persecution, bitter grief, pain, and death.

Before returning to His heavenly throne, Jesus underwent one more glorious change: resurrection from the dead on Easter morning. As a result of our Lord's change from death to life, we know beyond all doubt that the heavenly Father has accepted His Son's payment for our sin once and for all!

There is one more change left to be made: the change of our sin-sick bodies to perfectly glorified bodies on the day our Lord comes back to judge the earth. These bodies will be familiar to us in that they will truly be our bodies. But these bodies will also be very different from those we now have, because they will be perfect—perfectly healthy, without sin, and desiring everything God desires. Are you ready for the best part? Everyone who knows and loves the

Lord Jesus will be together with God and His angels in heaven forever.

This glorious change will occur either after we have died or, if we are alive on the Last Day, we will be changed "in the twinkling of an eye." Trusting this wonderful event is in our future, we want to make sure that our wives and children continue to hear these great promises of God made real in Christ through faithful worship in His Word and Sacrament. As we do, we eagerly look forward to this wonderful change!

Lord Jesus

I know how mortal I am. Keep me mindful each day of the change I will undergo in the resurrection. Help me resemble that new man now. In Your name. Amen.

Today's Challenge

Consider the bad habits in your mortal life. Pick one and ask the Lord for strength to change this bad habit into a good one.

The Goal of Real Maturity

When I was a little boy, I always wanted to do things that were about 10 years beyond my maturity level. One of my earliest memories is of ice fishing on Lake Minnetonka, on the western edge of the Twin Cities. For those of you who have never ice fished, it is important to know that after the hole in the ice has been drilled, you must scoop out the ice shavings before the baited hook, sinker, line, and bobber can slide down the hole.

My father has always been wise, and he knew better than to let me have the ice scoop. I, however, thought differently. Worn down by my insisting that he let me scoop out the ice, my mother finally said to my father, "Oh, let him try." No sooner did I have the ice scoop in my hand than it was swimming in the icy abyss.

This episode from my early youth lived on in infamy and is an example that we are naturally immature when we are young. We simply are not capable of doing the same things we can do when we are older. It is so important to learn at every stage of life that we have special jobs and responsibilities appropriate for whatever age we happen to be. Knowing that, and happily performing those responsibilities, are the keys to maturity. In today's lesson from St. Paul, we learn what real maturity is from God's vantage point. St. Paul wrote:

> It was [Christ] who gave some to be apostles, some to be prophets, some to be evangelists, and some to be pastors

and teachers, to prepare God's people for works of service, so that the body of Christ may be built up until we all reach unity in the faith and in the knowledge of the Son of God and become mature, attaining to the whole measure of the fullness of Christ.

Ephesians 4:11–13

St. Paul spoke of maturity not in terms of age, but as a goal made possible by Christ alone. Christian maturity is a lifestyle in which selfish, sinful desires are denied and the cross of Jesus is picked up and carried daily by the power of the Holy Spirit in our Baptism.

What is it to be mature in God's eyes? Cleaning up a child's vomit between the bed and the wall at 2:00 A.M.? Not arguing with our wives when they are feeling moody? Regularly helping out with the laundry, the dishes, and the meals? All of these are examples of maturity. But there is also the example of maturity you give by getting up on Sunday morning early enough to get your family dressed and on their way to church. Or saying bedtime and meal prayers with your kids, initiating home devotions, and talking about Jesus whenever the opportunity arises.

It is through Christ that we learn what real maturity is, since He displayed the ultimate in unselfish behavior toward us, His sinful children. Our Lord was completely humble and gentle when He stepped off His throne in heaven and entered the womb of the virgin Mary to become one of us. Jesus was patient and loving as He allowed people to accuse Him of casting out demons by the power of the devil, as He was hit in the face, as He was tortured with the Roman scourge, and as He was finally nailed to the cross. God in Christ put our needs ahead of His own, while so many looked on as though it was just a big joke.

When we consider His complete devotion to us, is God really asking too much of us when He desires that we put Him first in our lives? In light of all Jesus has done for us, does it not seem reasonable to put the needs of our loved ones and neighbors ahead of our own? As we continue to grow with our families "in the faith and in the knowledge of the Son of God" through faithful feeding on His Word and sacraments, we will—by the power of the Holy Spirit—"become mature, attaining to the whole measure of the fullness of Christ." God gives that kind of faithful maturity to all ages!

Lord Jesus

Even in times when my pride is wounded, help me put the needs of my wife, children, and others You have brought into my life before my own. Fill me with Your Holy Spirit so I may show myself to the world as one of Your mature sons. In Your name. Amen.

Today's Challenge

The next time your kids try to do something beyond their age, admire their gumption. Instead of saying no, try to find a way to do it with them.

Life in the U.S.A.

What if you had a friend who never lied to you, who always told you the truth without embellishing it for his own benefit. What if this friend always took care of you, putting your needs ahead of his own. What if, after a lifetime of proving to you how utterly trustworthy he was, you asked your friend: "What have you done for me lately?" or "Why should I trust you?" Surely everyone would think you were a fool.

As we mature, we learn how important it is to pick our friends carefully. A major criteria for choosing friends is whether they are trustworthy. Yet when we decide not to trust friends without having a good reason, or we turn away simply because they tell us something we do not want to hear, we are being very foolish indeed! And how much more foolish are we when we turn away from God and consider Him not worthy of our trust!

As you read today's Scripture, think about why God is so worthy of your trust. Think about why this devotion is titled: "Life in the U.S.A." St. Paul wrote:

> People will be lovers of themselves, lovers of money, boastful, proud, abusive, disobedient to their parents, ungrateful, unholy, without love, unforgiving, slanderous, without self-control, brutal, not lovers of the good, treacherous, rash, conceited, lovers of pleasure rather than lovers of God—having a form of godliness but denying its power. Have nothing to do with them.
>
> *2 Timothy 3:2–5*

This same warning St. Paul gave to Timothy applies to us today. We must remember that what we see going on in the world is by no means pleasing in God's eyes. As we read this catalogue of sins that typifies our world, we ought to sit up and take notice.

We need to ask ourselves: Am I a lover of myself? Of money? Am I boastful? Proud? Abusive? Disobedient (or disrespectful) to my parents as they are getting older? Am I ungrateful? Unholy in my lifestyle? Do I lack a loving attitude in general? Do I have problems forgiving other people their sins? Do I slander people to make myself look better? Do I choose not to control my sinful impulses? Am I brutal to others at times? Do good words and actions by others make me happy, or am I jealous (or even sickened by) the kindness and generosity of others? Do I ever take advantage of people? Does a personal accomplishment make my ego swell? Would I rather spend time scratching my sinful itches than studying God's Word and being about the things that please Him? Do I appear to be godly to my family, friends, and fellow church members, yet harbor doubts and suspicions about the trustworthiness of God and His Word in my life?

If this self-examination hits you hard with bad news, that's good! That is what the Law of God does. It accuses us and destroys the proud and arrogant attitude that is so natural to us all. Are you ready for some Good News? The words of St. Paul encourage us in our study of Scriptures. Paul said, "All Scripture is God-breathed and is useful for teaching, rebuking, correcting and training in righteousness, so the man of God may be thoroughly equipped for every good work" (2 Timothy 3: 16–17).

The Law of God is undeniably correct. By ourselves, we stand condemned. Thankfully, God comes to us with love that none of us deserves. He sent His Son to obey the Law in our place. Jesus offered up His life as the one perfect offering for our sins and those of the whole world. Through faith alone in the crucified and risen Christ, God no longer sees our sins. He distributes the precious gift of salvation to us through His Good News called the Gospel. God gives us salvation through our Baptism and the Lord's Supper. Since God has never lied to us, but instead completely reveals His love through His Son, our Savior, by His Holy Word, how can we listen to any other voice?

Paul's warnings of unscrupulous and underhanded people apply to all of us as we face life in the U.S.A. Let us pray for all who are tempted to love themselves more than God. Praise God that in Christ we have a Friend who will never lie to us. Jesus makes us wise for salvation through faith in Him!

Lord Jesus

Thank You for giving me the privilege to live in a country where I am free to worship You and enjoy the many freedoms I have. Make me a blessing to others in this land. Allow me to be Your light shining in a dark place. In Your holy name. Amen.

Today's Challenge

When you get frustrated at immorality and sinful attitudes, take a moment to pray for those involved. Feel compassion for their lost condition and pray for their salvation. Remember that Jesus died for that person as much as He died for you.

~~Been There~~, Done That; Now ~~Here~~, Doing This

It's interesting how we Americans come up with phrases as fashionable and trendy as any clothes we wear. We might say "You the man," which basically means "good job." In the '70s, to say something was "bad" meant that it was really good. Today, "the bomb" means the greatest, "nasty" still means nasty, and "been there, done that" translates into "I understand."

When it comes to understanding, no one understands better than God. We may be tempted to ask: "How does God understand what I am going through? After all, He is perfect, and I am a sinner. How could God possibly understand my troubles or sympathize with my shameful weaknesses?" Although God has never sinned, He assures us that through Jesus He does indeed understand. Jesus came to earth in human form, complete with physical frailties and emotions. Jesus experienced all of the daily trials and temptations we encounter.

We may even paint an idyllic portrait of the prophets and apostles who were given the privilege to work closely with the Lord in their lifetimes. It is no secret that a large number of Christians have imposed on these men a superior status over all other Christians. A closer look at Scripture, however, reveals quite a different picture.

Take St. Paul, for example. He was one of the most respected and prestigious Pharisees, university-trained under the feet of Gamaliel, the foremost Jewish teacher of that day. Paul, originally named Saul of Tarsus, was a young man full of zeal for the traditions of his fathers. As discussed in a previous devotion, he approvingly held the coats of those who stoned to death St. Stephen. Energized by that bloodletting, great persecution broke out against the Church. And Saul, breathing murderous threats against the believers in Christ, obtained letters from the high priest giving him permission to have Christian families broken up and thrown into prison.

Does that sound like a saintly past for one of God's great saints? Hardly! That is where today's lesson comes in. Paul was referring to himself when he wrote, "At one time we too were foolish, disobedient, deceived and enslaved by all kinds of passions and pleasures. We lived in malice and envy, being hated and hating one another" (Titus 3:3).

The phrase "at one time" means that "been there, done that" was part of Paul's life:

> But when the kindness and love of God our Savior appeared, He saved us, not because of righteous things we had done, but because of His mercy. He saved us through the washing of rebirth and renewal by the Holy Spirit, whom He poured out on us generously through Jesus Christ our Savior, so that, having been justified by His grace, we might become heirs having the hope of eternal life. This is a trustworthy saying.
>
> *Titus 3:4–8*

We see clearly that sainthood is not something that is bestowed on "super Christians," but rather it is a gracious, undeserved gift from God given to everyone who trusts in Jesus as his or her only Savior from sin. These words from Paul drip with mercy, kindness, and love. This gift of eternal life also drips from God in another most marvelous way: our Baptism! God's promises ring loud and clear in these words of Baptism, "[God] saved us through the washing of rebirth and renewal by the Holy Spirit." God has saved us through the death and resurrection of our Lord Jesus Christ. Now, through Baptism, God gives all who trust in Jesus the beautiful name *saint*. That means all of us who trust in Jesus as our Savior are going to heaven immediately when we die. It means that we can leave behind the "been there, done that" part of life and join Paul in the "now here, doing this" part of living as baptized, redeemed saints of God.

Lord Jesus

Through my Baptism, I am saved eternally. Help me live every day in the strength, joy, and peace of my rebirth until I see You face to face in heaven. In Your name. Amen.

Today's Challenge

Consider your own personal weaknesses. Rejoice that God has a place in heaven for you—not because you deserve it, but because Christ has bestowed His great mercy and love on you and your family in Baptism!

Overwhelming Fire Power

Have you ever wondered why police cars have a shotgun mounted in the front seat? If the policeman has a handgun strapped to his side, why does he need more weapons? If the officer already has a shotgun, why are there S.W.A.T. teams? Law enforcement officers hope and pray they will never have to use deadly force to take control of a situation. But if the situation requires, police officers want to make sure they have overwhelming fire power for the safety of both citizens and themselves.

No illustration is perfect, but there does seem to be a connection between the overwhelming fire power of a law enforcement officer and the metaphorical fire power of God's Word. God doesn't tell us only once what we need to know to be saved. His truth is so important for the human race, that He makes His salvation known time and again throughout the Bible. Keep this in mind as you turn to Hebrews chapter 11. Pay attention to how the Scriptures are stuffed with the message that we are saved through faith in Christ, not through good works:

> By faith the people passed through the Red Sea as on dry land; but when the Egyptians tried to do so, they were drowned. ... And what more shall I say? I do not have time to tell about Gideon, Barak, Samson, Jephthah, David, Samuel and the prophets, who through faith conquered kingdoms, administered justice, and gained what was promised; who shut the mouths of lions,

quenched the fury of the flames, and escaped the edge of the sword; whose weakness was turned to strength; and who became powerful in battle and routed foreign armies. Women received back their dead, raised to life again. Others were tortured and refused to be released, so that they might gain a better resurrection.

Hebrews 11:29, 32–35

People who do not trust God for their salvation either dismiss God's Word as myth or pay it all kinds of lip-service, calling it "a fine book of morality," "the greatest philosophy ever written," and so forth. The divinely inspired writer of Hebrews presented a very different reason for recording the miraculous events in the lives of these heroes. He wrote, "These were all commended for their faith, yet none of them received what had been promised. God had planned something better for us so only together with us would they be made perfect" (Hebrews 11:39–40).

The Bible unites us with these heroes of the faith in the saving grace of Jesus Christ. Only God can do the uniting. Only God could deliver these heroes of the faith from the Red Sea, the mouth of the lions, the fury of the flames, the sword's sharpened steel, torture, and even death. Only God could give these perfectly normal human beings the faith necessary to trust in Him through all they endured. Only God could come up with the plan to save us from sin, death, and the power of the devil forever in one decisive victory. When God's Son came into our world as true God and true man, He said, "But I, when I am lifted up from the earth, will draw all men to myself" (John 12:32).

When we trust in Jesus as our only Savior from sin, we are a hero of the faith by the power of the Holy Spirit. You may be thinking, *Huh? I'm no hero!* Fortunately, God knows we are uncertain of our abilities and has therefore armed us with His Word. The Bible is packed with the fire power of the true stories of the many different heroes of the faith: Noah, Abraham, Moses, David, Daniel, and the rest. The undeserved grace of God made them heroes, not their own worthiness (indeed, Moses pleaded with God to choose somebody else). God caused all these people to yearn for the heavenly home that was not yet theirs, but was coming because they trusted His promise.

God makes you a hero to your family so you can fulfill your personal responsibility to lead your wife and children to Jesus. That means going with them every week to worship, saying daily prayers with them, having devotions together, and setting a godly and loving example to these, the dearest people in your life. The Holy Spirit provides the "fire power" so God's gift of heroic faith in Jesus can be revealed through you to others. That is a real hero!

Lord Jesus

Thank You for including me among the people whom You have made heroes of faith in You! In Your name, Amen.

Today's Challenge

At your own pace, begin a lifelong project of getting to know the true stories of the Bible heroes mentioned in Hebrews chapter 11.

Consult The Daily Planner

I have a daily planner. Funny, but I haven't figured out how it works. Every time I open it, it's still blank. It hasn't once planned my day for me! If your daily planner works, maybe you could let me know what I'm doing wrong. As for today's devotional thought, we are directed by St. James to a much better approach to planning our days and our lives. James encourages us to consult God, the ultimate daily planner. James wrote:

> Now listen, you who say, "Today or tomorrow we will go to this or that city, spend a year there, carry on business and make money." Why, you do not even know what will happen tomorrow. What is your life? You are a mist that appears for a little while and then vanishes. Instead, you ought to say, "If it is the Lord's will, we will live and do this or that." As it is, you boast and brag. All such boasting is evil.
>
> *James 4:13–16*

With all of the scheduling and deadlines in our lives, it is extremely easy to lose sight of one important thing: nothing happens without the Lord allowing it to happen. James reminds us: "You who say, 'Today or tomorrow we will go to this or that city, spend a year there, carry on business and make money.' Why, you do not even know what will happen tomorrow." How often have you invested time and money into plans only to have to change them at the last minute because something unexpected happened? James warns us that *we* are not in control of the future. How foolish then, to boast and brag about what we will be doing and accomplishing! James tells us that all such boasting is evil.

God has a much better way for us to deal with our busy lives. He asks, "What is your life? You are a mist that appears for a little while and then vanishes. Instead, you ought to say, 'If it is the Lord's will, we will live and do this or that.'" How appropriate! God is eternal. Our lives are temporary—even compared to many forms of vegetation and animal life (trees, tortoises, and crocodiles often live longer than humans). How dare we be arrogant before God! Rather, let's commend our daily affairs into the hands of our Lord Jesus Christ who has taken care of our eternal affairs.

God's Son knows well the limitations of earthly time. He was born at just the right time. Then, in His limited time on earth, He lived a perfect life obeying all of God's laws and fulfilled each of the Old Testament prophecies. The most comforting fulfillment of the Old Testament was the suffering predicted by Isaiah in chapter 53:

> He was despised and rejected by men, a man of sorrows, and familiar with suffering. ... Surely He took up our infirmities and carried our sorrows, yet we considered Him stricken by God, smitten by Him, and afflicted. But He was pierced for our transgressions, He was crushed for our iniquities; the punishment that brought us peace was upon Him, and by His wounds we are healed ... and the LORD has laid on Him the iniquity of us all. *Isaiah 53:3–6*

Isaiah clearly expressed the New Testament Gospel under the Holy Spirit's inspiration nearly 680 years before Christ was even born. As our Lord was pierced by nails on the cross and later with a Roman spear, the punishment we deserved was paid in full by His bitter wounds and death. God is now at peace with us for Jesus' sake. His resurrection from the dead, also a prophecy kept, guarantees our resurrection on the Last Day. Thank God He did what He did in the fullness of *His* time.

What about our busy, scheduled lives? We can prioritize Sunday morning as time for worship around God's Word and precious sacraments. We can be careful to reserve enough time to enjoy our wives and our children. However, before making any plans, we ought to begin with prayer, making the phrase "Lord willing" second nature to our hearts and speech. That is how to faithfully consult God's Daily Planner in Jesus' name.

Father

It is so easy to think that my plans for the future are accomplished through my efforts. Forgive my arrogance. By Your Holy Spirit, daily direct me to look to You in Your Word for guidance to live within Your will for Your Son's sake. In Jesus' name. Amen.

Today's Challenge

In the upper corner of your daily planner, write "Lord willing" to remind you that the plans for today and all days will be accomplished according to God's will.

You Can Take This Job and ... Do What?

Have you ever been employed at a place where you felt like finishing the sentence in the title with a less-than-appropriate sentiment? Do you feel that way now? If now or in the past you have felt discouraged or frustrated with your job, this devotion is speaking to you. St. Peter wrote:

> Submit yourselves for the Lord's sake to every authority instituted among men. ... Live as free men, but do not use your freedom as a cover-up for evil; live as servants of God. ... Slaves, submit yourselves to your masters with all respect, not only to those who are good and considerate, but also to those who are harsh. ... To this you were called, because Christ suffered for you, leaving you an example, that you should follow in His steps. ... When they hurled their insults at Him, He did not retaliate; when He suffered, He made no threats. Instead, He entrusted Himself to Him who judges justly.
>
> *1 Peter 2:13–23*

Trusting that God's love frees us from sin means we can submit out of Christian love to all authorities—parents, spouse, pastor, teachers, governing officials, and even those insecure bosses who seem to enjoy abusing their authority. When we obey the authorities in our lives, we obey God. As undesirable as the word *submit* may be to our pride, through St. Peter God is pointing us to the greatest honor of all—imitating our Lord Jesus Christ.

Peter wrote, "To this you were called, because Christ suffered for you, leaving you an example, that you should follow in His steps." The world doesn't understand this, but we are actually drawn closer to Christ in two ways—in our faith and in our lives. Both of these are the work of God (Ephesians 2:8–10).

Our faith is the hand that lays hold of what Christ did for us in His suffering and death on the cross. In verse 24 Peter wrote, "[Jesus] Himself bore our sins in His body on the tree, so that we might die to sins and live for righteousness; by His wounds you have been healed." Christ has healed us from the guilt and fear of the divine punishment we deserve because of our sin.

You are free, by the blood of Christ, to serve your God. As you do so, another authority to whom you submit is your pastor, who is called to teach you the truth of God's saving Word, pronounce God's forgiveness on all who repent, baptize, and give the Lord's Supper to all who believe. All of these precious gifts Christ has given to us, His Church, for the forgiveness of our sins and the strengthening of our faith.

You are free, by the blood of Christ, to serve others, following in His footsteps. When bosses or coworkers hurl insults at us, following in our Lord's footsteps means that we do not retaliate. Likewise, when we suffer, we can pray for the people who persecute and torment us.

Perhaps your witness to the joy in your life might inspire others to want that joy for themselves and to find it in the saving grace of Jesus Christ. Through your example, may your children learn one way to finish this sentence: "You can take this job and … let me serve my God with it!"

Heavenly Father

Sometimes it is difficult to show respect and obedience to authorities who treat me poorly. Forgive me my weaknesses, and help me with Your Spirit's mighty power to hold my tongue and serve You by serving others. In Jesus' name. Amen.

Today's Challenge

Do your job so well that difficult bosses will not have a leg to stand on should they falsely criticize you.

Faith's Vitamins

Have you ever known people who are pill poppers? I'm not talking about a person whose health concerns require prescription drugs. I'm talking about people who take a variety of pills in an attempt to prevent this or that disease, or believe the pills make them stronger and healthier. Look at the many different vitamins on the market. A variety of herbal supplements are designed to improve memory or emotional balance, lower your cholesterol, or raise your sex drive.

Although many consider pills to be the quick-fix answer to problems, nutritionists tell us that vitamins in pill form often do not deliver the full supply of nutrients our system needs. Nutrients are often flushed out before they are absorbed by the body. Even if taken consistently, earthly vitamins are not a miracle cure.

But through regular doses of God's Word and frequent trips to the Lord's Table, God works an internal difference in our faith that is demonstrated in God's Word for today:

> For this very reason, make every effort to add to your faith goodness; and to goodness, knowledge; and to knowledge, self-control; and to self-control, perseverance; and to perseverance, godliness; and to godliness, brotherly kindness; and to brotherly kindness, love. For if you possess these qualities in increasing measure, they will keep you from being ineffective and unproductive in your knowledge of our Lord Jesus Christ. But if anyone does not have them, he is nearsighted and blind,

and has forgotten that he has been cleansed from his past sins.

2 Peter 1:5–9

Faith in Jesus alone cleanses us from our past sins, our present sins, and even our future sins. Here St. Peter writes about the qualities of a healthy faith.

Each of these qualities hinges on the one before it like a wonderful spiraling-upward effect. Peter starts with goodness. The next step flows from simple goodness to knowledge. A good and faithful child of God will want to know more about the God in whom he believes. This means attending worship weekly, going to Bible study as much as possible, and nurturing a healthy devotional life. From knowledge in God's Word flows self-control. The meaning is simple, but the applications are endless. Whatever your personal weakness—wandering eyes, gossiping, a quick temper, alcohol abuse, or whatever else—God restrains those sinful appetites as His Holy Spirit gives us strength through His Word and Sacrament.

From self-control comes another equally useful weapon against Satan's attacks: perseverance. I can't help but think of a rigorous exercise program. It really hurts to push our muscles and do more reps with more weight. But in the first two weeks of bench pressing, the lactic acid is worked out of the system and we are able to "key up" the stack to the next weight. We find that what was impossible before is now possible. Likewise, it really hurts to resist sin and take abuse from a world hostile to God. Yet God uses the very things we hate in life to make us stronger in Him. The consistent, God-pleasing lifestyle perseverance provides is what the Bible calls *godliness*. From godliness flows brotherly kindness.

One who is godly has passed through many fires in this life, has grown in knowledge of God's love for him through His Word, and has a genuineness of character that views others as special for the sake of Christ. Knowing that God wants all people to be saved, even those rascals in our life, is reason enough to treat all people with kindness that goes far beyond basic goodness or decency. This heartfelt desire for all people to be saved is the true meaning of Christian love.

While earthly vitamins are quickly flushed out of our system, God graciously promises that consistent feeding on His Holy Word and Holy Meal will continue to nourish our faith to new levels of eternal health and everlasting longevity.

Lord Jesus

Never let me forget that all my sins are forgiven. By the power of Your Holy Spirit through Your Word and sacraments, may these qualities of faith grow in an ever-increasing measure until I am perfect in heaven. In Your holy name. Amen.

Today's Challenge

Keep your vitamin bottle next to your Bible to remember to feed on His Word and dine at His Table.

Take It from the Eyewitnesses

A criminal trial might take days, weeks, or even months, and a variety of types of witness can help establish the accused's guilt or innocence.

Two types of witnesses are character and expert. The defense or prosecution can use both to help prove their case. Neither was anywhere near the crime scene when the crime took place. Even so, the court views their testimony as valuable because of some specific knowledge these witnesses have relating to the case. (Call me old-fashioned, but if I were a judge or juror in a court of law, I'd prefer an eyewitness to an expert witness any day.)

As we turn to Holy Scripture, we find that the apostles had to deal with those who would seek to twist the truth. St. Peter assures us that he and his fellow apostles knew what they were proclaiming. They were not merely character or expert witnesses for Jesus. They were *eyewitnesses* of those things the Lord Jesus did on earth. St. Peter wrote:

> We did not follow cleverly invented stories when we told you about the power and coming of our Lord Jesus Christ, but we were eyewitnesses of His majesty. For He received honor and glory from God the Father when the voice came to Him from the Majestic Glory, saying, "This is my Son, whom I love; with Him I am well pleased." We ourselves heard this voice that came from heaven when we were with Him on the sacred mountain.
>
> *2 Peter 1:16–18*

Some truth twisters say the Bible is just a book of human stories and myths. Many believe Bible stories cannot be true because they don't have definitive proof that the people existed or the events took place. However, if we lived our lives not trusting anything we did not make or do or see, we would never cross a bridge or use an elevator.

Trusting people and their workmanship every day enables us to function without undue fear. We trust the engineers who designed the bridges over which we drive and the elevators in which we ride. We trust the people who design and maintain the airplanes, the automobiles, and the amusement park rides in which we travel.

If we are willing to entrust our lives and those of our family to engineers and construction workers we have never met, how much more should we trust our lives and our souls to the one true God whom we confess engineered and still preserves our bodies, the glorious world, and the entire universe. We witness God's marvelous handiwork every day in the wonders of creation and the beauty of our fellow human beings. We are blessed daily with the love and forgiveness Jesus graciously earned for us through His death on the cross.

Just before Jesus died on the cross, our Lord took the inner circle of His disciples—Peter, James, and John—to the top of a mountain, and there they saw Jesus' appearance change from normal to as bright as the sun. Then Moses, representative of the Old Testament Law, and Elijah, representative of the prophets, appeared and talked with Jesus. Peter said, "Lord, it is good for us to be here. If you wish, I will put up three shelters—one for You, one for Moses and one for Elijah" (Matthew 17:4). Then a cloud enveloped them and Peter heard the words of the heavenly Father, "This is My Son, whom I love; with Him I am well pleased" (Matthew 17:5).

Through the power of the Holy Spirit, I place my trust in my Lord and Savior Jesus Christ. I am moved by testimony of the divinely inspired eyewitnesses to believe in the death and resurrection of God's Son. Call me old-fashioned, but I prefer an eyewitness account any day.

Lord Jesus

Through Your chosen eyewitnesses, I see Your majestic glory. Help me to view Your Word with eyes of faith, trusting its truth for the salvation of my family's souls. In Your name. Amen.

Today's Challenge

Share the eyewitness account in today's reading with someone who does not know Jesus.

The Year 2000? Big Deal!

In the last months of 1999, there were outrageously priced celebration packages at world-class hotels, expensive cruise vacations, and other "once in a thousand years" opportunities planned around a momentous millennial event. Some, however, stockpiled food and supplies, believing that the year 2000 would bring mass chaos and destruction. Still others feared that the end of the millennium might give way to the end of the world.

Early in the morning on January 1, 2000, as Dick Clark finished his "Rockin' New Year's Eve" television special, the world was still intact. Nothing destructive happened. Some said, "See! I told you nothing would happen!" But wasn't God the only one who actually knew what the new millennium would bring? To say, "See! I told you nothing would happen!" without faith in the Lord is not at all different from the attitude Noah faced as he built the ark under a clear blue sky. Most likely, Noah was a laughing stock for all the years he and his family worked on the great vessel. Nobody was laughing, though, when the floodwaters covered the mountains.

Concerning the non-event of the millennium, some may still say, "See! I told you!" But instead of saying it with arrogance and insolence, this statement can be uttered with profound fear and respect by people who acknowledge the Lord alone as God. Such people know what the Bible has to say about the end of the world. They know that God is not moved by numbers on humankind's calendar. God's children can faithfully say, "Y2K? Big deal!" St. Peter wrote:

> First of all, you must understand that in the last days scoffers will come, scoffing and following their own evil desires. They will say, "Where is this 'coming' He promised? ..." But they deliberately forget that long ago by God's Word the heavens existed and the earth was formed out of water and by water. By these waters also the world of that time was deluged and destroyed. By the same Word the present heavens and earth are reserved for fire, being kept for the day of judgment and destruction of ungodly men. ... [The Lord] is patient with you, not wanting anyone to perish, but everyone to come to repentance.
>
> *2 Peter 3:3–9*

Those who disregard God's promise to come back are fools. God said they "deliberately forget" all that He teaches through His Word. Yet God waits in patience, not wanting anyone to perish.

There is so much to digest in today's Scripture about how the world will end. The world was first destroyed by a worldwide flood during the time of Noah. God made the rainbow as a lasting reminder of His promise that He would never again destroy the earth by water. Now that Jesus has come to earth, died on the cross, rose again, and returned to heaven, the universe is officially in the last days of which Peter spoke.

After the unleashing of God's power on Good Friday and Easter, the only cataclysmic event that remains is Christ's return on Judgment Day. On that day, Christ will raise all the dead, destroy the earth and all the created elements, and take us to heaven to be with Him forever.

Until that great day, the Holy Spirit empowers you to live in humble preparation for our Lord's return and also commissions you to tell everyone the Good News about Jesus. God is God. He doesn't have to prove He exists to anyone. As you remain focused on the task at hand, ignore the distractions unbelievers throw your way and confidently say, "Y2K [or any other year] is not a big deal. Let the Lord's will be done."

Lord Jesus

When I am tempted to listen to those who scoff at Your Second Coming, help me, by the power of Your Holy Spirit, to remember Your promise of faithfulness. Give me the courage and strength to witness Your love to my family and those around me. In Your name. Amen.

Today's Challenge

Next time you see a tabloid in the check-out line that predicts the end of the world, consider this: those who deny Holy Scripture are just as lost as those who think the world will end by a UFO attack. Pray for those who do not yet know Christ and the truth of His Word.

Don't Kid Yourself

When I was in college, my roommate and I, along with the other guys on our dorm floor developed our own language. The large African knife fish in my roommate's aquarium was *the Hodge. Chix* meant wonderful, and *I don't believe you* translated into *Don't kid yourself! Don't kid yourself!* was the phrase used by far the most. It came in handy when we wanted to save one another from little white lies and embellished truths.

You know that living in truth is always better than living in a lie. Living a life of lies in relationship to others is dangerous and destructive. Trust is broken, feelings are hurt, and relationships are destroyed. How much more dangerous, then, is living a life of lies in relationship to God? How many times have you thought *I am not a sinner*? Or, *My sins aren't that bad*. For those who think along these lines, St. John says, *Don't kid yourself!:*

> If we claim to be without sin, we deceive ourselves and the truth is not in us. If we confess our sins, He is faithful and just and will forgive us our sins and purify us from all unrighteousness. If we claim we have not sinned, we make Him out to be a liar and His Word has no place in our lives.
>
> *1 John 1:8–10*

Many dads have caught at least one of their kids red-handed doing something wrong. Although dad has proof in hand, and there are eyewitnesses everywhere, the child still struggles to deny guilt. She swears she didn't get paint on the table as she holds the dripping brush in her hand. Knowing the frustration of dealing with people who try to cover up misdeeds and even serious sins, how can we possibly try to cover up our sins before God? He sees and knows everything, even the secrets deep in our hearts.

Rather than trying to cover up the sinful jams into which we place ourselves, today's passage reads, "If we confess our sins, He is faithful and just and will forgive us our sins and purify us from all unrighteousness." Do dads actually enjoy disciplining their children? No. They'd much rather ask them to do something and have them obey. God the Father does not enjoy punishing sin either. However, He is a just God who cannot ignore sin. God simply wants us to stop kidding ourselves. He wants us to admit our sins in our hearts, and then confess them to Him. Most important, God wants us to trust that He has forgiven these and all our sins for the sake of His Son, Jesus Christ.

God forgives us and purifies us from all our unrighteousness. God loves to welcome sinners whose sins have been washed away in the blood of His only begotten Son, Jesus Christ. Since Christ died for us and the whole world, there is no reason for anyone to ever kid themselves by thinking or saying they are not sinners. Through Jesus' blood we are washed clean. Christ has prepared a place in heaven for all of His redeemed children. Christ's sin-cleansing blood was showered on us when we were baptized into saving faith in Jesus through the power of the Holy Spirit.

Through faithful worship with your family, hearing His Word, and being united with Christ through His body and blood, may God work through you to be honest with Him and with one another until that day you are taken to heaven, never again to face the temptation to kid yourself.

Lord Jesus

Help me to never kid myself concerning my sins. Preserve within me, by the power of Your Holy Spirit, a firm understanding of the great debt of love I owe You. I can never repay You for Your death on the cross for my sake. Thank You for blessing me with undeserved mercy and grace. In Your Holy name. Amen.

Today's Challenge

If there is a wrongdoing you have not admitted to your wife, do it today. Seek her forgiveness. Pray that the Holy Spirit would guide your words and actions, as well as open your wife's heart to forgiveness and reconciliation.

Spiritual Teflon

During the 1980s, some said that President Ronald Reagan was made of Teflon, that legendary nonstick coating. Accusations the news media and politicians threw at him just wouldn't stick. Some believed he could do no wrong. As we well know, however, no human being is perfect. The Teflon coating wears away and the flawed surface beneath shows through. Reagan's blameless reputation was eventually marred by the Iran-Contra affair. Similarly, everyone eventually shows their imperfect traits. Yet God covers the flaws time and again with the forgiveness that is ours through Christ.

Consider the life of the apostle Peter. He denied he knew Jesus the night Jesus was on trial for His life. Even so, following our Lord's death and resurrection, God gave Peter great courage to proclaim Christ as the Savior of the world. Although he once tried to keep the accusation of being Jesus' disciple from sticking, Peter later took great joy in being stuck to that same blessed name. Through Peter, God tells us that although the whole world may accuse us of evil, God has robed us in Christ's righteousness and strength, our own spiritual Teflon. Peter wrote:

> Dear friends, I urge you, as aliens and strangers in the world, to abstain from sinful desires, which war against your soul. Live such good lives among the pagans that, though they accuse you of doing wrong, they may see your good deeds and glorify God on the day He visits us.
>
> *1 Peter 2:11–12*

Have you ever given someone advice only to be told, "That's easy for you to say!"? That reply suggests that you are out of touch with the other person's problems. Thankfully, God is never out of touch. Peter's urging to abstain from sinful desires and to live good lives amid accusations of wrongdoing is familiar to Jesus. He knows exactly what it's like to live on earth.

Jesus took human flesh and lived in our world. Our Lord understands the pull of temptation, the pain of self-restraint, the exhaustion attached to doing what is right, and the anger of being falsely accused by jealous and selfish people. As true God and true man, Jesus Christ was pure perfection through and through, yet out of love He allowed our sins to stick to Him so He might take them to the cross.

Jesus was stuck with all our filthy thoughts, our self-serving words, and our neglectful actions and attitudes, as well as God's just hatred against these and all sins, and the curse of death itself. Jesus dragged Himself and our sin as He carried the cross to Calvary. As He hung bleeding, naked, and in unimaginable torture, the Father poured out every last ounce of His divine anger onto His beloved Son. This is why Jesus cried out, "My God, My God, why have You forsaken Me?" (Matthew 27:46).

Jesus died to take away all our sins and rose so we might have everlasting life. Through our Baptism, we have died with Christ and have been raised with Him to new life (Romans 6:1–7).

Christ became sticky with all our sin so we could, by the power of His Holy Spirit in His Word and sacraments, be renewed in Baptism and be covered time and again with His love and forgiveness. The good news is that even when others throw false accusations at us, the covering of

God's grace is His binding promise that those world accusations will never stick.

Lord Jesus

I am a weak and sinful man. Have mercy on me. Forgive my sins, and in the peace You give me through my Baptism, help me give great honor and glory to Your holy name. Let those who do not know You come to know You through the power of the Holy Spirit. In Your name. Amen.

Today's Challenge

Make scrambled eggs for supper tonight using two pans. Make half the eggs in a regular stainless steel frying pan, and the other half in a Teflon-coated pan. Which do you prefer? Think about how God has covered you with Teflon in Christ, in a world sticky with sin.

The Standard

What do you think of when you hear the word *standard?* To refer to something as "the standard" is to say it is that against which all others must be compared. With pride, a manufacturer states that their product or service "sets the *standard* for quality and excellence." Even in an age of rising prices, American consumers make it clear that they are willing to pay a high price for high quality. But while consistently demanding high quality from others, we often forget that we fall short of perfection.

The good news is that God has "standardized" His love for us in Jesus Christ. By trusting in His grace and mercy, God gives us the gift of a new standard for living our lives as His people. St. John wrote:

> This is the message you heard from the beginning: We should love one another. ... This is how we know what love is: Jesus Christ laid down His life for us. And we ought to lay down our lives for our brothers. ... Dear children, let us not love with words or tongue but with actions and in truth. ... Those who obey His commands live in Him, and He in them. And this is how we know that He lives in us: We know it by the Spirit He gave us.
>
> *1 John 3:11–24*

Until the day our Lord Jesus returns, humankind will continue to struggle with the relationship between saving faith and good works. It is part of human desire to want to claim at least some credit for salvation. Few are so bold as to flat-out say, "I am saved by own good works." Most will admit that God has done most of the work necessary to save us, but there's always a "but"—some kind of condition that does not let the Gospel rest on good news alone. One example of a conditional phrase is, "Sure, Christ died for the guilt of our sin, but we must satisfy the punishment of our sin in purgatory." Or, "Jesus died on the cross to take away all your sins. It's a free gift, but first you must make a decision to accept Jesus as your Savior and invite Him into your heart."

Neither approach reflects the Gospel as presented in Scripture. With God, there are no conditions. The question of conditions boils down to two great teachings in the Bible: Law and Gospel. These two must be kept completely separate when presented, taught, and applied to each individual.

The Law demands God's perfect standard from each of us under threat of eternal punishment. The Gospel, on the other hand, makes no demands of us whatsoever. The Gospel proclaims the Good News that God's Son, Jesus Christ, has come to earth to be our perfect standard by His perfect life. Through Jesus' perfect life and His sacrificial death, He delivered the goods: forgiveness of sins, deliverance from death and the power of the devil, eternal peace with God in heaven, earthly and eternal joy, the Father's ear to all our prayers, and all other blessings. Truly He is your standard, and you are saved by faith alone!

Then where do good works come in? Husbands and fathers have received God's ultimate gift of love in Christ. By the power of the Holy Spirit working through your Baptism, His Word, and the Lord's Supper, good works are the evidence of your faith, a reflection of Christ in your life. You are not saved by your love of God or others; rather, you love because you are saved. God's new standard is ours through Christ.

Lord Jesus

Thank You for becoming my Standard before the heavenly Father. Remind me every day that by Your perfect life, death, and resurrection, You have given me the only standard I need to live by as Your disciple in this imperfect world. In Your name. Amen.

Today's Challenge

Next time you drive past a Standard Oil Company sign, or see a bathroom fixture labeled Standard American, remember the standard Christ met for you.

Final Exams

Ask students what part of class they dread the most, and they will likely say "final exams." Why? Because final exams cover everything that has been taught from day one. To prepare for a final exam, students have to dig through past notes, trying to draw out concepts and theories embedded in their memories to prove they have mastered the course material. Teachers don't give exams because they get some kind of sadistic joy in watching their students sweat nervously. Teachers use exams to determine how much truth or error their students have retained regarding the course material.

In a sense, we take exams in our life's experiences too. When a man leaves his father and mother and is joined to his wife, they find out how much they learned when they were under the care of their parents. When a seminarian is ordained and installed in his first congregation, an examination begins of how much he learned about true theology and the care of souls while he was in the classroom, in his fieldwork, and during vicarage.

Today's devotion tells us that distinguishing truth from error is the most critical exam we will ever experience—the final exam. St. John wrote:

> Dear friends, do not believe every spirit, but test the spirits to see whether they are from God, because many false prophets have gone out into the world. This is how you can recognize the Spirit of God: Every spirit that acknowledges that Jesus Christ has come in the flesh is from God, but every spirit that does not acknowledge

Jesus is not from God. This is the spirit of the antichrist, which you have heard is coming and even now is already in the world ... We are from God, and whoever knows God listens to us; but whoever is not from God does not listen to us. This is how we recognize the Spirit of truth and the spirit of falsehood.

1 John 4:1–6

In our high-tech world, we are constantly bombarded with people's voices, many of which come from the unbelieving world around us. Although much of what we hear is useful, many voices endeavor to lead us away from God: *All religions are simply different roads that lead to the same place; Come on, we all know Jonah was never really swallowed by a big fish; Jesus was a great moral teacher and philosopher—even a great prophet—but nothing more; Mary was likely made pregnant by an itinerant Roman soldier; Jesus was likely buried in a shallow grave and eaten by dogs.*

These kinds of falsehoods come from the false prophets St. John warned against. If deceived by the spirits who do not acknowledge Jesus, we risk losing the very salvation Christ purchased for us with His precious blood.

God has provided a way for us to stand firm against the test of false teachings, and that is through trust in Jesus alone for salvation from sin, death, and the power of the devil. In Mark 16:16 we read, "Whoever believes and is baptized will be saved." Here's another easy one to remember, "I am the way and the truth and the life. No one comes to the Father except through Me" (John 14:6).

Another good verse to remember is John 10:27–28, "My sheep listen to My voice; I know them, and they follow Me. I give them eternal life, and they shall never perish; no one can snatch them out of My hand."

And finally, "We are from God, and whoever knows God listens to us; but whoever is not from God does not listen to us" (1 John 4:6).

With all the misleading voices in the world competing for our ear-time, it is of supreme comfort to us to know that the one Voice we can trust is that of Jesus. He has demonstrated His trustworthiness through His death on the cross and the gift of His Holy Spirit in Baptism. He continues to unite Himself to us through His body and blood. God has completed our final exam in the blood of Christ. That is the saving truth your wife, children, and rest of the world need to hear from you!

Lord Jesus

Through Your prophets and apostles, You have warned us repeatedly against false prophets. When I see and hear others attack You, remind me that this is just one more part of Your Holy Word that has come true. Give me strength to always trust Your Word so I will never be deceived. In Your name. Amen.

Today's Challenge

Consider other religions of the world that are Law-based. Their version of salvation is focused on something we must do. Rejoice that salvation is Gospel-based. It is not based on what we must do, but solely on what Christ Jesus has already done, and continues to do, for us!

Me? A Priest?

To many in our world, the title *priest* means only three things: no sex, no fun, and lots of boredom. Knowing that I am a pastor, some of my son's friends once asked, "How did you get here? Isn't your dad a priest?" My son's friends were thinking of the belief that requires clergy to take a vow of celibacy. They didn't realize that pastors can actually get married! My son's friends also didn't realize that they, themselves are priests.

In today's lesson, the apostle John records a personal message from our Lord Jesus Christ to us His Church in Revelation 1:1–3. Paraphrased, His message is "Be ready! My return is very near. Until that day I have work for you to do." St. John wrote:

> The revelation of Jesus Christ, which God gave Him to show His servants what must soon take place. ... Blessed is the one who reads the words of this prophecy, and blessed are those who hear it and take to heart what is written in it, because the time is near. ... To Him who loves us and has freed us from our sins by His blood, and has made us to be a kingdom and priests to serve His God and Father—to Him be glory and power for ever and ever! Amen.
>
> *Revelation 1:1–6*

The word *priest* is loaded with meaning. In Old Testament times, the tribe of Levi was the priestly tribe among the 12 tribes of Israel. They were not allotted a geographical area of the Promised Land because their portion was the privilege of serving Him day and night in His temple. The role these priests performed was threefold: 1. They were to speak God's Word to the people, teaching the congregation; 2. They were to offer sacrifices to God for the sins of the people; and 3. They were to make intercession, or pray, to God on behalf of His people.

The New Testament book of Hebrews identifies our Savior Jesus Christ as our "great High Priest." As our great High Priest on earth, Jesus proclaimed the Good News of salvation through God's Word and miracles that verified all that He preached. Regarding the second role of a priest, Hebrews says, "Day after day every priest stands and performs his religious duties; again and again he offers the same sacrifices, which can never take away sins. But when this Priest had offered for all time one sacrifice for sins, He sat down at the right hand of God" (Hebrews 10:11–12).

Only by the precious blood of God's Lamb, His only Son, are all our sins paid for, washed away, and cancelled forever. Instead of offering sacrifices time and again like the Old Testament priests, Jesus sacrificed Himself only *once.* The final role our great High Priest serves will continue until He returns to take us to heaven as He prays to the Father on our behalf: "For there is one God and one Mediator between God and men, the man Christ Jesus" (1 Timothy 2:5).

What else does God have in store for us? Turning to the Scripture from St. Peter, we hear this wonderful declaration from God, "But you are a chosen people, a royal priesthood, a holy nation, a people belonging to God, that you may declare the praises of Him who called you out of darkness into His wonderful light" (1 Peter 2:9).

Remember the opening thought from Revelation? Time is running out. How then does God enable us to serve Him as His own priests? First, He empowers us to speak His Word to everyone we know. Second, we offer intercessions, or prayers, to Him on behalf of others. Third, we offer ourselves and our entire lives to Him as "living sacrifices" (Romans 12:1). Thanks to the saving work of God in your life, you can answer the question "Me? A Priest?" with the response "Yes, I am."

Lord Jesus

You alone are my great High Priest. Help me to speak Your Word faithfully, pray for the needs of others, and offer myself to You each day as a living sacrifice. Help me by the power of Your Holy Spirit. In Your name. Amen.

Today's Challenge

Beginning with this prayer, make a conscious effort to fulfill the three roles of priesthood that Christ bestowed upon you through Baptism. Be assured that you are special to God.

Read Psalm 144
Revelation 21:1–27

WHY SETTLE FOR
A PIECE OF REAL ESTATE?

When I was growing up, my parents had a cabin in central Minnesota. The sight of sunlight peeking through jack pines swaying in the wind, the "knock-knock" of the occasional woodpecker, the smell of lake water mixed with a little gasoline, and the distant sound of a boat motor are memories permanently imprinted on my brain and heart.

There are many happy family memories tied to that cabin. One night my sister opened her cot and uncovered a nest of baby mice. Grandma Pfaffe stayed up half the night with a broom in her hand, waiting for the mama mouse to come out from under the steps. I remember the Fourth of July my soon-to-be brother-in-law brought his St. Bernard to the fireworks display. At the first boom, the dog dragged him back to his car, leaping over the front seat, disappearing from sight.

As precious as these memories are to me, there were unseen burdens that accompanied owning the cabin: expenses for property taxes and utilities, money for fuel to transport us back and forth every weekend, and the cost of routine maintenance such as lawn care and upkeep. Those of you who own property are well acquainted with the commitment and burdens that often tarnish the pleasure of ownership.

When it comes to eternal life, why would we ever settle for a piece of real estate on this earth? Why do so many people believe that Jesus will establish an earthly reign in the city of Jerusalem when He returns? As we turn to the very end of the Bible, we find that the new Jerusalem God is preparing for us is not the Jerusalem across the ocean, but a glorious, heavenly Jerusalem. St. John wrote:

> Then I saw a new heaven and a new earth, for the first heaven and the first earth had passed away, and there was no longer any sea. I saw the Holy City, the new Jerusalem, coming down out of heaven from God ... And I heard a loud voice from the throne saying, "Now the dwelling of God is with men, and He will live with them. They will be His people, and God Himself will be with them and be their God. He will wipe every tear from their eyes. There will be no more death or mourning or crying or pain, for the old order of things has passed away."
>
> *Revelation 21:1–4*

After reading this passage, there are some observations we can make about the paradise we will enjoy after we die. The first observation is that human language cannot capture all that our heavenly home will be. Our human minds cannot fathom a world without pain and death. Although we can dream about such a world, we cannot truly understand or express what it will be like until we finally experience it.

The second observation is that God gives us just enough of a picture to keep us focused on our heavenly home and not on the things of this world. The city of Jerusalem had great importance for the Old Testament people of God. It was the city of King David, whose throne would one day be occupied by the coming Savior of the world. Jerusalem's most significant feature, however, was that the Lord of heaven and earth made His dwelling in the Most Holy Place in the temple at Jerusalem. When Jesus, the Son of God, entered the temple to teach, the Scripture recorded by the prophet Malachi was fulfilled. Malachi wrote, "Then suddenly the Lord you are seeking will come to His temple ... " (Malachi 3:1).

Our Lord arrived in Jerusalem to purchase our salvation. He lived the perfect life we could not live because of our sin. He voluntarily went to the cross just outside the city walls of Jerusalem and there suffered our eternal punishment. By our Baptism into Jesus' precious blood shed for us on the cross, we have received a perfect washing away of all our sins. Through faith alone in Jesus, we are made citizens of the new Jerusalem which God is preparing for us this very minute!

We look forward to the day when we will see the new, heavenly Jerusalem. We will rejoice that God has made all things brand new for us, having taken away all death, crying, and pain. Our future heavenly residence comes free of all burdens and personal expense. Jesus' loving sacrifice has paid our bills in full.

Lord Jesus

Thank You for making everything in my life new. I have been reborn in Holy Baptism and am daily renewed by the forgiveness of Your precious blood. I anxiously await my new home in heaven. Help me never lose sight of all I already have and have yet to look forward to with You. In Your name. Amen.

Today's Challenge

Whether you own property or rent, ask yourself this: Is this (your earthly home) paradise? Thank God for the real home waiting for you in heaven.

Part II:

The Husband in the Family

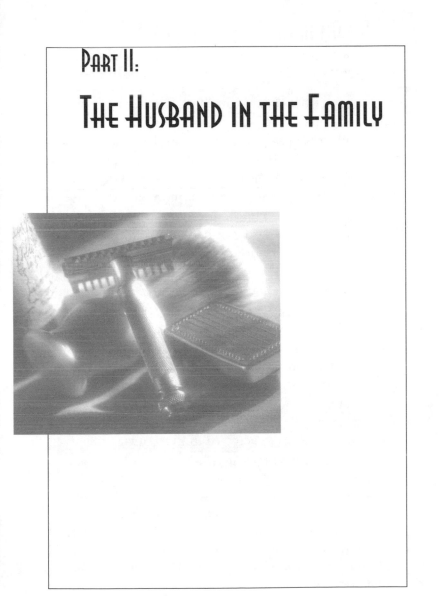

Read Proverbs 4
Genesis 1

It's All in the Image (His Image)

Not long after our oldest son Mark was born, an elderly lady commented, "You can sure tell you're the father!"

"Thank you," I said, while my mind added an unspoken, *I think*. Now, 11 years later, as I watch my son and three other beautiful children grow up, it gives me great joy to see that they resemble both mom and dad. As my wife and I watch our children mature, the resemblances they bear to Debbie and me have ups and downs. For example, when the children are behaving well or demonstrating great talents, Debbie will say they are *her* children. When they are misbehaving or embarrassing themselves, she informs me they are *my* children.

It is natural for parents to view their children's behavior as a personal reflection of them. When children are acting well, parents are proud. When children misbehave, parents are embarrassed. If sinful human beings care about the image their children reflect on them, it should not surprise us that God cares about His image reflected in us. In Genesis chapter one, we read that God created us in His image:

> Then God said, "Let Us make man in Our image, in Our likeness, and let them rule over the fish of the sea and the birds of the air, over the livestock, over all the earth, and over all the creatures that move along the ground." So God created man in His own image, in the image of God He created him; male and female He created them. God blessed them and said to them, "Be fruitful and increase in number; fill the earth and subdue it."

Genesis 1:26–28

Whereas the rest of creation was made by the word of God alone, man was made in a special way: "the LORD God formed the man from the dust of the ground and breathed into his nostrils the breath of life, and the man became a living being" (Genesis 2:7). God breathed into man His own life-giving Spirit, giving him an eternal soul, the gift of human reason, and the image of God. The image of God was simply this: man knew God as God wanted to be known. Man was perfectly happy by nature living in obedience to God.

After creation, God placed Adam in a garden called Eden, where He also created a helpmate for Adam. Adam and Eve were perfectly happy and free to do whatever their hearts desired, as long as they obeyed God's single command not to eat the fruit from the tree of the knowledge of good and evil. This tree established the relationship between Adam and God, reminding man that he was God's creation—not the other way around. God desired their love and trust for Him be expressed in terms of their obedience.

This image was horribly lost when Eve, and then Adam, elected to eat the forbidden fruit. Having been deceived by the devil, they believed they could become more like God. With that taste, they learned the difference between good and evil; they learned about evil and death. Although our first parents did not fall over on the spot, death indeed entered their bodies and all creation. Worst of all, they were dead in their perfect relationship with God.

God banished Adam and Eve from the garden as a consequence of their sin. But at the same time, in His boundless love, compassion, and mercy, He made a promise. At the same moment He confronted Adam, Eve, and the devilish serpent, God made a promise to send a Savior from sin who would "crush [the devil's] head" (Genesis 3:15b). The offspring of the woman who would crush the devil was the Son of God, our Lord Jesus Christ.

Through His perfect life on earth, Jesus held sin, death, and the power of the devil captive in His suffering and death on the cross (Romans 5:12–19). By the same creating power of His Word and in the waters of Baptism, God the Holy Spirit creates faith in our hearts to trust in Jesus as our Savior. Our old sinful nature has been drowned.

In your Baptism, God claims you as His own and begins the restoration of His image in you, which will come to completion in eternity. Praise God that it's all in *His* image.

Heavenly Father

By the power of Your Holy Spirit, help me show the restored image You have begun in me through the precious blood of Jesus. In Jesus' name. Amen.

Today's Challenge

Next time your children are acting like *your* children, discipline them with love. Consider how you are reflecting your heavenly Father's image.

GOD KNEW WE NEEDED A WIFE

Not long after the excitement of the wedding settles down, there come those days of stresses, moods, and fears that can tempt men to look at their new role and think, *I don't need this.*

For every time you have said or thought something like that, consider this: God always knows best. In fact, He didn't give you just one hole in your head, He gave you five holes in your head: two nostrils, two ears, and a mouth. God always knows what's best for us. The same principle applies to marriage.

Just as God knew best when He gave us holes in our heads, God knew best when He blessed men with help-mates—their wives! As you read Genesis chapter two, you will discover how God has demonstrated His love by bless-ing you with a lifelong companion.

Before Eve was created, all the birds, fish, and land ani-mals filled the earth. And there was Adam. God put Adam to work right away naming all the animals God had made. Each creature had its own mate. "But for Adam no suitable helper was found" (Genesis 2:20).

> So the LORD God caused the man to fall into a deep sleep; and while he was sleeping, He took one of the man's ribs and closed up the place with flesh. Then the LORD God made a woman from the rib He had taken out of the man, and He brought her to the man. The man said, "This is now bone of my bones and flesh of my

flesh; she shall be called 'woman,' for she was taken out of man." For this reason a man will leave his father and mother and be united to his wife, and they will become one flesh.

Genesis 2:21–24

Everything was perfect except for one thing: Adam needed a companion. God chose to make Adam's companion a woman, creating Eve from Adam's rib. He used a part of Adam's own body as a reminder to husbands and wives of their intimate connection. Moses testified in Genesis that God's joining of Adam and Eve was the very first wedding ceremony. When sin entered the world through Adam and Eve, God promised to send a Savior, placing Christ in the center of their union. Only through the power of the Holy Spirit can husband and wife remain in this relationship as God intends. With Christ at the center, each spouse is daily washed in the divine forgiveness of Holy Baptism. Because of this divine forgiveness, the couple is empowered by the Holy Spirit to live in a state of forgiveness toward one another.

The apostle Paul used the relationship between Christ and His Church as the model for husbands and wives. He wrote, "Husbands, love your wives, just as Christ loved the church and gave Himself up for her to make her holy, cleansing her by the washing with water through the Word ..." (Ephesians 5:25–26). Having been washed in the blood of Christ shed for you on the cross, and having received that washing in your Baptism, you can now look at your wife as the precious gift from God that she truly is. She is perfect, cleansed of all sin through the same washing you have received in Christ. Indeed, God *knew* you needed a wife!

Father

Thank You for blessing me with my wife. Help me follow the example of Christ, caring for her needs as well as the needs of my children. Allow Your Holy Spirit to lead them to Jesus, so their burdens in this life may be easier to bear. In Jesus' name. Amen.

Today's Challenge

Next time you feel frustrated with something your wife says or does, think about what your life would be like without her. Thank God He has given you such a wonderful blessing!

Blaming Our Wives Is Nothing New

Humans are quick to take credit for their accomplishments. But are they just as quick to accept the blame for their failures? Hardly. Why? For the answer, we need to go back to Adam and Eve. Pay attention to what happened right after our first parents disobeyed God by eating the fruit from the tree of the knowledge of good and evil:

> But the LORD God called to the man, "Where are you?" He answered, "I heard You in the garden, and I was afraid because I was naked; so I hid." And He said, "Who told you that you were naked? Have you eaten from the tree that I commanded you not to eat from?" The man said, "The woman You put here with me—she gave me some fruit from the tree, and I ate it."
>
> *Genesis 3:9–12*

Realizing we have done something foolish is frustrating and often frightening. We become angry at the person who holds us accountable because we are embarrassed, guilt ridden, and defensive. In a way, we feel naked and vulnerable when accused. We are tempted to blame anyone other than ourselves. We often blame those who accuse us. Sometimes God even gets the blame for letting us be stupid. Sadly, all too often our wives bear the brunt of our blame because they are closest to us and may even be most likely to point out our foolish behavior.

Adam and Eve's disobedience brought God's curse of pain, toil, and death upon the earth. The good news is that God has never stopped being the gracious, loving, and patient God that He is. We see God's searching love immediately after humankind fell into sin. Although God knew where Adam and Eve were as they hid, God still asked "Where are you?"

God still asks "where are you?" when we wander away from Him in sin. God made a promise to Adam and Eve that day in the words of condemnation aimed at the serpent: "I will put enmity between you and the woman, and between your offspring and hers; He will crush your head, and you will strike His heel" (Genesis 3:15). Jesus Christ was Eve's offspring who finally crushed Satan through His holy death and resurrection some 2,000 years ago.

We can now afford to admit all of our sins, confident of the full forgiveness of Jesus Christ. This forgiveness brings us peace with God and restores joy in our relationships, especially our relationships with those who share our faith in Jesus. Being quick to admit to our sins and refusing to blame others sets a powerful example of strength in the Lord that we pray our loved ones will follow.

Instead of blaming others for our failures and sins, we can turn to God and humbly ask His forgiveness. God's forgiveness is not an abstract idea. God's forgiveness actually cleans up the messes our sin makes in our relationships with other people as well as in our relationship with God. As you gather with your lovely wife and children in God's house around His Word and Holy Communion, God takes away your blame, forgives all your sins, and assures you that He is no longer angry with you for Jesus' sake. Although blaming our wives is nothing new, by the Spirit's Power, we can make it something old!

Dear Lord Jesus

Give me the strength I need to assume responsibility for my own sin. Give me the strength to be humble and confess my sins, trusting they have all been paid for by Your precious blood shed on the cross. In that joy, let me live in peace with my wife, children, and all with whom I live and work. In Your holy name. Amen.

Today's Challenge

"Blame" your wife today for the good things God has given to you through her.

God Is Good for His Word

Credit cards are extremely easy to get. Because creditors want a large customer base, they freely distribute credit cards among the general population. Companies invite the masses to an introductory membership, and then weed out those who cannot keep up with their payments.

A customer that does not get caught in the credit card trap is one that makes his payments on time. He's the kind of person who doesn't spend beyond his means. This kind of customer possesses a valuable quality. He is a person who is good for his word.

Yet even people who are good for their word can vary in their trustworthiness. They can go from having good to bad credit, then back to good because of unfortunate circumstances or poor decision-making. God, however, is always good for His Word. This fact will become abundantly clear as you read about the lives of Moses and the Israelites.

> You were shown these things so that you might know that the LORD is God; besides Him there is no other. From heaven He made you hear His voice to discipline you. On earth He showed you His great fire, and you heard His words from out of the fire. Because He loved your forefathers and chose their descendants after them, He brought you out of Egypt by His Presence and His great strength, to drive out before you nations greater and stronger than you and to bring you into their land to give it to you for your inheritance, as it is today.
>
> *Deuteronomy 4:35–38*

In Exodus 1–3, we see God's hand in the miserable lives of the descendants of Jacob (Israel). The Israelites were enslaved by an Egyptian pharaoh who did not know God. The order was given throughout Egypt that every Israelite baby boy be thrown into the Nile, but the mother of one put him into a basket and sent him down river where he landed near Pharaoh's daughter as she bathed. God stirred the heart of Pharaoh's daughter with compassion, and she adopted the boy as her own, calling him Moses. God used Moses' unique position as both an Israelite and the prince of Egypt to make Moses God's greatest Old Testament prophet.

When Moses fled for his life to the land of Midian, God spoke to Moses from the burning bush on Mount Sinai. God called Moses to go back to Egypt and tell Pharaoh to "let [God's] people go" (Exodus 5:1). After the Lord enabled Moses to perform many signs, wonders, and the 10 awful plagues—and after the angel of death had killed all of the first born Egyptian males—the hard-hearted Pharaoh finally let the Israelites leave Egypt.

God's fulfillment of His promise to free Moses and the Israelites and bring them to the land He promised Abraham offers some of the greatest proof that God is always good for His Word. As Israel was gathered on the east side of the Jordan River, following their 40-year wilderness wandering, Moses reminded them of every promise God had made. Moses told them that crossing over and taking possession of this promised land was proof that God would always be faithful and save His people. God would remain with them forever. From that day on, whenever Israel needed strength to trust the Lord, all they needed to do was remember how God delivered them out of slavery in Egypt.

The God who fulfilled His promise to Israel is the same God who fulfilled His promise to deliver us from our slavery to sin, death, and the power of the devil. Through Christ's death and resurrection, we will live with Him forever. Our promised land is heaven.

Let us encourage our wives and children on the path to the promised land of heaven as we faithfully continue to lead them to worship. Because God is good for His Word, He strengthens our faith in Christ and continues to wash away our sins in Holy Baptism and the Lord's Supper. Thank God that our salvation does not depend on our own effort or credit rating for, good customer or not, we would always fall short.

Heavenly Father

You always keep Your promises. Help me remember Your faithfulness. Enable me to trust Your promises, especially Your promise to forgive all my sins and take me to heaven. In Jesus' name. Amen.

Today's Challenge

Next time you get a pre-approved credit card offer, look for the asterisk after the low introductory rate. Pay attention to what the fine print really tells you. Thank God that His promises don't have fine print. God is always good for His Word!

God Loves to Work against the Odds

In recent decades, America has experienced a proliferation of gambling. You're fortunate if you can find an hour of television programming that does not include a commercial for a lottery game or a casino. What makes these games and places attractive? Although the food and entertainment at casinos offer incentive to visit, perhaps the most inviting draw rests in the message of a billboard I once saw: "A good, clean place to get filthy rich." However, the odds of a person walking away filthy rich are not as great as the advertisement suggests.

Casinos and lotteries are not the only places where the idea of *odds* is used. The idea describes the probability or chance of a certain outcome occurring. When good things happen, we often hear "How lucky!" When bad things happen, we're likely to hear "How unlucky!" These comments are so common they are difficult, even for Christians, to avoid. Speaking of luck shows how common it is for people to view life as a result of chance and odds.

In Luke's gospel, we meet Zechariah. He and his wife, Elizabeth, were very old and Elizabeth was barren. Zechariah had been chosen to burn incense in the temple. While there, an angel of the Lord told him Elizabeth would give birth to a son. The angel said:

> "Do not be afraid, Zechariah; your prayer has been heard. Your wife Elizabeth will bear you a son, and you are to give him the name John. ... Many of the people of Israel will he bring back to the Lord their God." ...

Zechariah asked the angel, "How can I be sure of this? I am an old man and my wife is well along in years." The angel answered, "... now you will be silent and not able to speak until the day this happens, because you did not believe my words, which will come true at their proper time."

Luke 1:13–20

In the first chapter of Luke, we read that the priests cast lots to determine who was supposed to enter into the Holy Place of the temple to offer incense while the faithful gathered outside to worship. The lots fell in Zechariah's favor, and the Archangel Gabriel appeared to announce the coming birth of a son to Zechariah. God chose Zechariah to go into the Holy Place where he would receive this good news.

Gabriel's good news wasn't simply the news that one elderly, barren woman and her elderly husband were going to conceive a child. Although this indeed was a miracle, there was much more to Gabriel's announcement. The Lord was on His way to earth—in the flesh! The long awaited Messiah, the Savior of the world, was about to set foot on our earth. And Zechariah's miracle baby would be the Savior's forerunner, announcing to the world that Jesus of Nazareth was the Son of God.

In Baptism, through water and the Holy Spirit, God has adopted you, your wife, and your children into His own family. The guilt and punishment of your sins have been washed away and paid for in Christ's blood, shed for you on the cross. Our Savior's resurrection from the dead is God's personal guarantee that nothing about your salvation has been left to chance. Since you have a God who has made your salvation a sure thing in Christ, may you, with His Spirit's power, turn away from everything that looks at life as lucky and unlucky. May you commend yourself and your family into the hands of your gracious God who loves to work against all odds for His people.

Heavenly Father

Remind me every day that You demonstrate Your mighty power and salvation in ways I don't always expect. Give me an extra measure of Your Holy Spirit through Word and sacraments so I may always trust Your promises of love. In Jesus' name. Amen.

Today's Challenge

If you have a pair of dice handy, pick them up. Look at them, then rejoice that God never left any part of your salvation up to chance.

HEARING IS CHEAP

How many times have you heard the phrase "talk is cheap"? That means it's easy to talk big, but quite another thing to back up those words with action.

God, who is always truthful and faithful, out of His great love for us, comes down to our level and backs up His word with the great wonders and miracles recorded in both the Old and New Testaments. We know God's talk is never cheap. That's not the issue. The issue is our *response* to God's true Word. In our Gospel lesson from Matthew, we realize that truly hearing God's Word leads to action. St. Matthew wrote:

> "Therefore everyone who hears these words of mine and puts them into practice is like a wise man who built his house on the rock. The rain came down, the streams rose, and the winds blew and beat against that house; yet it did not fall, because it had its foundation on the rock. But everyone who hears these words of mine and does not put them into practice is like a foolish man who built his house on sand. The rain came down, the streams rose, and the winds blew and beat against that house, and it fell with a great crash."
>
> *Matthew 7:24–27*

Any parent who knows the frustration of talking to his children until he is blue in the face, only to have his children act as if he hadn't said a word, can picture what Jesus is saying to us today. To merely listen to the Word of God without putting it into practice would be as foolish as the builder who thought that sand would provide a firm foundation.

As you study God's Word, however, you find it filled with evidence that points to the fulfillment of His promises to you and to me. A wise man builds his house on *that* Rock—the foundation of God who speaks and keeps His Word.

God sent His Son to declare us forgiven of all sin. Righteousness is ours because our Lord Jesus Christ gave us His righteousness when He died on the cross for every sin we have committed and for the guilt and punishment we deserved. Through faith alone in Jesus, God has declared all of us not guilty for the sake of His Son.

Through faith in Jesus, the Holy Spirit creates a new life within our hearts that desires to please God with righteous living. God enables us to put the words of our Lord into practice. He gives us strength to give the Lord and His Word first priority in our lives. Built on the solid foundation, the rain can come down, the streams can rise, and the winds can blow and beat against our house, but we will not be destroyed. God is true to His Word. Listen and tell others!

Lord Jesus

Help me, by the power of Your Holy Spirit, to always be a doer of Your Word and not a hearer only. In Your name. Amen.

Today's Challenge

Each time you read or hear a portion of God's Word, pick out one or two things to put into practice. Remember that the wisdom to know and the strength to do this come only through the Holy Spirit, so begin with prayer.

DENIAL

We live in a mixed up world. A rapidly growing number of people dabble in non-Christian religions, while at the same time remaining members of a Christian church. With this growing interest in spirituality, one might conclude that our nation is concerned about their relationship to God. This, however, is not necessarily true. Much of today's "God talk" is not consistent with God's Word, trying to relate to God on man's terms.

Because of sin in our world, there are many conditions and crises that add to the mix up. We find ourselves in many forms of distress, looking to counselors and mental health experts for guidance and support as well as learning a whole new vocabulary.

One term from this vocabulary of psychological terms is *denial,* used to describe a person's refusal to acknowledge the truth regarding a particular situation. Today's lesson from Matthew's gospel exposes the worst form of denial that exists. St. Matthew wrote:

> A servant girl came to [Peter]. "You also were with Jesus of Galilee," she said. But he denied it before them all. "I don't know what you're talking about," he said. ... Another girl saw him and said to the people there, "This fellow was with Jesus of Nazareth." He denied it again, with an oath: "I don't know the man!" After a little while, those standing there went up to Peter and said, "Surely you are one of them, for your accent gives you

away." Then he began to call down curses on himself and he swore to them, "I don't know the man!"

Matthew 26:69–74

Sin is scary to the Christian. It is scary how easily sin catches us off guard. One minute we think we are doing God's will, living the way God wants us to. The next minute we are facedown in the mire of our sin. Consider the great apostle Peter. In Matthew's Gospel, Jesus told Peter that he would deny Him that very night. Peter boldly replied, "Even if I have to die with You, I will never disown you" (Matthew 26:35).

After his bold declaration, a servant girl struck terror in Peter's heart when she identified him as a disciple of Jesus. He was so filled with fear that he denied knowing our Lord with oaths and curses upon himself (Matthew 26:69–74). Perhaps that is why the Holy Spirit inspired Peter to later write, "Be self-controlled and alert. Your enemy the devil prowls around like a roaring lion looking for someone to devour. Resist him, standing firm in the faith" (1 Peter 5:8–9).

To sin against the Holy Spirit and to deny what Christ has done is the worst form of denial. Such a person is blind, spiritually dead, and an enemy of God. Jesus said, "But he who disowns Me before men will be disowned before the angels of God" (Luke 12:9).

Thanks be to God that Jesus came to die on the cross to save us from all our sins—including all the times we have denied knowing Jesus by our words and actions. Jesus never denied knowing us, although we are sinners. Hebrews 2:11 says, "Both the One who makes men holy and those who are made holy are of the same family. So Jesus is not ashamed to call them brothers." Such is the incredible love God has for us!

As we lead our families to the Word of God and His means of grace through regular weekly worship, the Holy Spirit promises to keep our faith in Jesus strong. He will also build within us such great confidence and courage in the Lord that we will be able to confess Jesus to the glory of God the Father before all people. He will bring us to a new vocabulary where denial does not exist—the vocabulary of the Good News of eternal life in Jesus.

Lord Jesus

Have mercy on me and forgive me all my sins. I know I am forgiven by Your gracious death on the cross. Please give me the courage and strength to speak and act in ways that show others I belong to You. In Your name. Amen.

Today's Challenge

The next time you hear someone well versed in psychological terms, share your Christian vocabulary with him.

Read Psalm 119:97–104
Luke 24:13–35

———

The Ultimate Bible Study

One frustration I experience as a pastor is the collection of preconceived notions many have about Bible study. Many consider Bible study boring because it includes history. Some think it is intimidating because they fear reading aloud or may not know the answer to a question. Others have been turned off by ineffective teachers.

Yet for some, Bible study is a real joy—a joy that comes from learning more about God and what His Word reveals.

When people are put off by Bible study, God's Word is never at fault. Satan fights hard to keep us from getting close to God's Word, lest His Word actually influence the way we believe, think, and live our lives.

In today's gospel lesson, negative notions about worship and Bible study are washed away. In their place we find that where God and His Word are, there is also real joy and excitement! As we look at the "ultimate Bible study" our resurrected Lord gave on the road to Emmaus, we see why study of God's Word is so important for every disciple of Jesus.

Two men met a stranger on the road, not realizing He was really their risen Savior. When they were about to part ways with Him, the two invited the stranger to stay with them. St. Luke wrote:

> So [Jesus] went in to stay with them. When He was at the table with them, He took bread, gave thanks, broke it and began to give it to them. Then their eyes were opened and they recognized Him, and He disappeared

from their sight. They asked each other, "Were not our hearts burning within us while He talked with us on the road and opened the Scriptures to us?" [Then] they got up and returned at once to Jerusalem.

Luke 24:29–33

Read today's lesson from Luke chapter 24. Imagine two people so downtrodden that their feet can barely drag them home. They are sad and confused. They cannot figure out what all the events of the last few days mean in God's plan of salvation. The crucifixion of their Lord Jesus seems like a senseless tragedy. Without Jesus, the world is hopeless. Then a stranger appears and begins walking with them. (Strangers often traveled together since robbers usually targeted those traveling alone.)

The stranger asks these two what they are talking about. They respond by stopping dead in their tracks. They cannot believe this stranger is unaware of what has happened in Jerusalem the last few days. Indeed the trial and crucifixion of Jesus must have rocked the whole city and its suburbs. They tell the stranger about Jesus and their hope that He was going to be the One to redeem Israel from sin. Then they share the bewildering news of the women who claimed that Jesus is alive!

The stranger replied, "Did not the Christ have to suffer these things and then enter His glory?" (Luke 24:26). We know the rest of the story. Jesus revealed Himself to the two disciples at the dinner table, then disappeared. Imagine how quickly their feet carried them those seven miles back to Jerusalem! If our Lord was able to use the Old Testament Scriptures to reveal that the Messiah's mission was to suffer and die for the sins of the whole world, how much greater the blessing that we have both Old and New Testaments!

God's Word is a treasure. It is so readily accessible, however, that we must fight with all our hearts the temptation to devalue it or take it for granted. The Bible is God's own inspired Word that clearly testifies to His love in Christ. His love is revealed in His saving acts throughout our world's history—from creation, to our Lord's death and resurrection, to His mighty acts performed in the ministry of His apostles and evangelists. These revelations prepare us for the second coming of our Savior Jesus who will raise us up with brand new bodies on the Last Day. Knowing that God draws us closer to Himself through His Word, how can we not want to see God revealed to us through the study of Scripture?

Lord Jesus

As You made the hearts of Your disciples burn within them by revealing Yourself through Scripture, give me Your Spirit that I might desire to know more about You as revealed through Your Word. In Your holy name. Amen.

Today's Challenge

If you are not already attending Bible study, encourage your wife to attend one with you. If you already attend, invite a friend to join the two of you. If your church does not offer Bible study, ask your pastor about starting one.

A Chosen Instrument

I have helped my sons make six Pinewood Derby cars. Any dad who has participated in the Cub Scout Pinewood Derby knows that the race itself is only icing on the cake. The real experience behind this race is the construction of the car. For me, this construction is no small task, as I am not known for my tool collection. In fact, any tool I do possess has been passed to me from my dad or father-in-law. Because my tools are few, I've often had to use them for jobs for which they were not intended, attempting to turn them into all-purpose tools.

Thankfully, God is much better at choosing tools or instruments to perform the jobs He wants done in His kingdom. As we consider the conversion of St. Paul, we marvel over the power of God in our lives to make all of us His chosen instruments. St. Luke wrote:

> As [Saul] neared Damascus on his journey, suddenly a light from heaven flashed around him. He fell to the ground and heard a voice say to him, "Saul, Saul, why do you persecute Me?" "Who are You, Lord?" Saul asked. "I am Jesus, whom you are persecuting," He replied. "Now get up and go into the city, and you will be told what you must do."
>
> *Acts 9:3-6*

Saul was the best of the best. He was the elite among his Pharisee colleagues, the religious leaders of the Jews. Saul wanted to please the God he thought he knew by keeping the Ten Commandments and the additional 600 man-made Jewish laws. He thought that was God's will.

Saul did not believe Jesus was the Son of God. After witnessing St. Stephen's execution for his faith, Saul was thirsty for the blood of all who believed in the death and resurrection of Jesus Christ. He thought he was performing the greatest service ever to the Lord by going after every man, woman, and child who called on the name of Jesus. The early Christian church never imagined that Saul would confess the religion he mercilessly persecuted.

Anyone who can look at the piles of junk in their garage and envision them turned into a tidy workshop can appreciate those television shows where a craftsman takes an unlikely tool and uses it to fashion a set of beautiful dovetailed drawers. God loves to do the same thing with people. He takes the most unlikely people and uses them to fix the worst situations imaginable.

After knocking Saul off his high horse of pride before God, the Lord Jesus called out from heaven in a blinding light, "Saul, Saul, why are you persecuting Me?" Without wasting a second, our Lord dispatched Saul to the house of a disciple upon his arrival in Damascus.

When the disciple Ananias was contacted by our resurrected Lord to go and baptize Saul, he reacted with the same fear we all would have felt. Our Lord reassured him saying, "Go! This man is My chosen instrument to carry My name before the Gentiles and their kings and before the people of Israel. I will show him how much he must suffer for My name" (Acts 9:15–16).

The rest is glorious history as we read about Paul's missionary journeys in Acts. God inspired His apostle to write numerous letters declaring the Gospel so we, and the rest of the world, could know Christ the Savior!

Jesus' perfect life and death on the cross earned our salvation. This salvation is ours through the waters of our Baptism, in His true body and blood in the Lord's Supper, and in His written Word, the Bible. God uses humans as His chosen tools to extend His kingdom throughout the world. Husbands and dads can never thank God enough for the privilege He has given them to be His chosen instruments to teach their wives and children about His all-purpose tool when it comes to loving us—the cross of Jesus Christ.

Lord Jesus

Thank You for displaying Your mighty power to change the hardest of hearts as You changed the heart of Saul. Remind me that You have called me in my Baptism to be Your chosen instrument where I live and work. Help me lead my family and those whom I know to You. Help me do this by the power of Your Holy Spirit. In Your name. Amen.

Today's Challenge

Every time you grab a tool, think about why you chose that tool over another. Remember how God has chosen you to do a specific job in His kingdom.

God's Wisdom Does Not Require a Diploma

Do you have a high school diploma? A diploma from a vocational or technical college? A two-year associate's degree? A bachelor's degree? A master's? A doctorate? Two doctorates? There are typically two ways people react to these kinds of questions. Some feel good about their level of education, proud of their formal training, schooling, or work experience. Others may feel ashamed or intimidated by those who have racked up more diplomas or titles than they currently have.

A truly wise person will tell you there is more to knowledge than formal schooling. Having a degree under our belts may be beneficial, but that certificate hanging on the wall is only as good as the person who earned it. Wisdom is a far more precious and rare commodity than the accumulation of knowledge.

Wisdom is a gift from God. Thankfully, God's saving wisdom does not require a diploma! St. Paul wrote:

> For the message of the cross is foolishness to those who are perishing, but to us who are being saved it is the power of God. ... Where is the wise man? Where is the scholar? Where is the philosopher of this age? Has not God made foolish the wisdom of the world? ... For the foolishness of God is wiser than man's wisdom, and the weakness of God is stronger than man's strength.
>
> *1 Corinthians 1:18–25*

I enjoy watching science documentaries. I marvel over the brilliance of God in creating our world with perfect design. However, as soon as I really start getting into the program, the narrator injects a comment like "The giraffe's long neck evolved when its ancestor, the horse, could no longer find food on the ground." It really frosts me when I hear evolution presented as a fact rather than the theory it really is.

The theory of evolution came out in the 19th century as an attempt to explain the origins of life and the universe apart from the existence of God. Today the scientific community is having enormous difficulties with evolution. Evolutionists are trying to force the newly discovered complexities of life into their outdated evolution model. Even James Watson and Francis Crick, the team that discovered the DNA molecule in 1953, reasoned that the blueprint for all life was too complicated to have come about randomly by an accident of evolution.

Such scientific trivia demonstrates the world's foolishness. The world may try to make you feel naïve for believing God's Word completely. Yet if every word of the Bible is true, why does it not get the respect it deserves?

St. Paul answered that question in the passage from 1 Corinthians. The world at large does not believe God's Word because humankind is sinful and considers Christ crucified foolish. The beauty of God's wisdom, however, is that while the world mocks Christians for their belief, God graciously ushers into His kingdom those who believe in Him with humble, childlike faith. Faith in God's Son Jesus Christ is wisdom humans cannot generate on their own, but can receive only by the power of the Holy Spirit through the Word of God, Baptism, and the Lord's Supper.

The message we communicate of Christ crucified for the sins of the whole world is fact—not theory. We know that the suffering, death, and resurrection of Jesus Christ is our only way to the Father through faith alone—not through scientific evidence. All who have this saving trust in Jesus for the forgiveness of sin are given the glorious title of "wise."

By the power of the Holy Spirit, we have the wisdom we need to put salvation of our wives and children first in our plans to care and provide for them. Let us lead them faithfully to worship and Bible study for the sake of Jesus Christ. That is the wisdom no diploma on earth can match.

Lord Jesus

By Your Holy Spirit in Baptism, You have given me Your saving wisdom. Keep me fed by Your Holy Word and sacraments all the days of my life so I might stay wise, looking to You alone for the forgiveness of sins and eternal life. Give me courage to tell others about Your love, beginning with my wife and children. In Your name. Amen.

Today's Challenge

If you have a diploma or some other symbol of a job well done, look at it and thank God for the gifts and talents He has given you. If you have your Baptism certificate, look at it and thank God for the gift of wisdom that no university on earth can offer.

Don't Get Cocky with God

Have you ever been attacked by a rooster? I once came close. As the proud male chicken fiercely defended the hens in his territory, I got into my car feeling a little foolish. After all, I had just backed down to a chicken. I was still impressed, however, by the courage this rooster showed against a creature almost 10 times its size. I wouldn't be surprised if the term *cockiness* originated from the rooster's proud strut and irrational courage.

Cockiness might be fine for roosters as they ward off intruders, this same trait is not so admirable in us if it stems from personal, sinful pride. As we continue with St. Paul's study of wisdom vs. foolishness, we learn that the ultimate in foolishness is to get "cocky" with God. St. Paul wrote:

> God chose the foolish things of the world to shame the wise; God chose the weak things of the world to shame the strong. He chose the lowly things of this world and the despised things—and the things that are not—to nullify the things that are, so no one may boast before Him. It is because of Him that you are in Christ Jesus, who has become for us wisdom from God—that is, our righteousness, holiness and redemption.
>
> *1 Corinthians 1:27–30*

There is a wonderful truth about God that humankind will never understand on its own: God loves to respond to sin by producing an opposite result. God made a perfect world and universe in the beginning. Sin brought death and suffering upon the earth. God responded with a promise to send a Savior. Israel thought the Savior was for Israel only, but God sent His only Son, Jesus, to die on the cross to redeem the sins of the whole world!

There is still one more wonderful opposite in God's great plan to save the human race. That opposite is how we enter the kingdom of heaven. Humans think God is impressed with physical beauty, strength, intelligence, philosophical wisdom, and other things people value. God, on the other hand, rejects the proud and the arrogant who trust in themselves and put their faith in worldly beauty and material gain. Instead, God tells us that faith in Jesus Christ as Savior is the only admission requirement for heaven.

It is human nature to strut around, boasting about ourselves every opportunity we get. But it is God who purchased our salvation through the blood of His Son Jesus. God did it, not us. And it is God who works one more opposite in our lives. He turns our self-centered boasting into a life that shows His great love to others.

The Holy Spirit will continue to squeeze out our self-absorption through God's precious Word and the Lord's Supper as we keep our eyes on Jesus and encourage our wives and children to do the same. He replaces our cockiness and self-centered boasting with a desire to brag about Him and all He has done for us in Jesus!

Heavenly Father

Remove me from my self-absorption. Fill me, by the power of Your Holy Spirit, with tremendous joy in You, that I may never boast except in the cross of Christ. In Jesus' holy name. Amen.

Today's Challenge

Do you know folks who take the credit for their own salvation? How might you boast in the cross of Christ to them?

Read Psalm 12
1 Corinthians 2:1–5

Single-mindedness

One of the television shows I really enjoyed in the 1980s was *Magnum, P.I.* There's one skill Magnum employed in the pilot episode I try hard to keep in mind when I'm faced with life's many distractions. This skill is single-mindedness.

In the pilot episode Magnum demonstrated his covert sneaking ability acquired as a U.S. Navy Seal. Magnum's mission was to enter his caretaker's compound by slipping past two Doberman pinschers, then unlock the door of the caretaker's sports car. Just when it seemed Magnum was free and clear, the dogs noticed him from across the large estate and bolted straight for the private investigator. Magnum kept repeating, "Work the lock, work the lock, don't look at the dogs, work the lock." Finally, with the dogs nearly upon him, the door opened. Magnum jumped inside, closed the door, fired up the engine, and peeled out of the driveway with a victorious grin.

I am not applauding Magnum's ability to break into and hot-wire a car. I am applauding his focus under intense pressure. As children of God, we have more threatening hounds snapping at our heels than those that pursued Magnum. Paul demonstrates a single-mindedness that will help us keep our eyes focused on Christ, even as we are constantly harassed by the devil, this world, and our own sinful flesh. St. Paul wrote:

> When I came to you, brothers, I did not come with eloquence or superior wisdom as I proclaimed to you the testimony about God. ... My message and my preaching were not with wise and persuasive words, but with a demonstration of the Spirit's power, so that your faith might not rest on men's wisdom, but on God's power.
>
> *1 Corinthians 2:1–5*

One of the great benefits of Bible study is discovering the background for the Scripture passage being studied. In this passage, Paul wrote to the Christians at Corinth, a major sea port in ancient Greece.

When a person thinks of ancient Greece, names of philosophers like Socrates, Plato, and Aristotle come to mind. Philosophy was highly valued by the Greeks. To be taken seriously and be respected, it was necessary to express one's philosophical position with great persuasion and polished oratorical skills, or rhetoric. Many times the winner of philosophical debates was decided not so much on the basis of their ideas, but on their presentation and persuasiveness.

St. Paul shattered this Greek emphasis on rhetorical skills when he proclaimed Jesus Christ crucified. God the Holy Spirit used St. Paul's weakness, fear, and trembling to prove that his message was not the same old philosophical rhetoric. Because there was nothing attractive in Paul's presentation, according to human standards, the fact that people were coming to believe in Jesus Christ proved that God—not Paul—was accomplishing salvation for these people. Indeed, Paul was very single-minded when it came to His message, "For I resolved to know nothing while I was with you except Jesus Christ and Him crucified" (1 Corinthians 2:2).

When it comes to our lives—whether in our role as husbands, fathers, employees, employers, church members, volunteers, or so forth—we too need to be single-minded about Whom we are really serving in every role we fill. Although it looks like we are only performing tasks for our wives, kids, bosses, or fellow members of Christ's body, we are also serving our Lord Jesus Christ. The ultimate Servant, He gave His life for us on the cross and rose again so we too will rise to everlasting life on the Last Day.

The devil, the world, and our own sinful flesh will try to distract us from trusting in Jesus and from doing what pleases God. They will even tempt us to give it up and start looking out for only ourselves. With the aid of the Holy Spirit, however, God enables us to focus on "working the lock without looking at the dogs." The Holy Spirit comes to us with this divine strength through faithful, weekly worship. Gathered with our wife and children around God's precious Word and His Body and Blood, God will use us to show others His magnificent power in our lives. That's a demonstration no rhetoric can beat!

Lord Jesus

There are so many things surrounding me that distract my focus away from You. Help me by the power of Your Spirit to keep this resolve: Every day, I will trust in nothing but You and Your death for my own salvation and that of my family. In Your precious name. Amen.

Today's Challenge

Think about how unimpressive the waters of Baptism appear. Consider how God purposely set it up that way so His saving power would be demonstrated through plain water combined with His most powerful Word.

Read Psalm 127
1 Corinthians 3:10–17

Built for Life

In the early 1960s, my father and mother watched our home being built from foundation to completion. Boy, did my dad watch! Evening after evening he would walk through the house, checking on the progress.

On one of those evenings, he was inspecting the fiberglass insulation between the studs. As he pressed against the paper backing, he felt nothing on the other side of the paper. He tore the paper back, and found no insulation! He ripped all the paper away to reveal an empty space, then he wrote a note telling the workers to add insulation.

Years later, a neighbor commented on the draftiness of his home. Yet our home remained nice and warm, thanks to my dad's diligence.

In today's Scripture reading, the building project is God's temple, His Church. In these verses, we are portrayed as the contractors and builders. The foundation has already been laid, but we have some important decisions to make concerning the quality of the building materials. What's it going to be, brothers, solid insulation or deceitful paper hiding an empty space? St. Paul wrote:

> By the grace God has given me, I laid a foundation as an expert builder, and someone else is building on it. But each one should be careful how he builds. For no one can lay any foundation other than the one already laid, which is Jesus Christ. If any man builds on this foundation using gold, silver, costly stones, wood, hay or straw,

his work will be shown for what it is, because the Day
will bring it to light. It will be revealed with fire, and the
fire will test the quality of each man's work.

1 Corinthians 3:10–13

It is no secret that not all who call on the name of
Jesus hold to exactly the same teachings. In any given
community across America, many different denomina-
tions within Christendom are represented. Each denomi-
nation has its own distinct position on the Scripture's
teaching called *doctrine.*

The fact that one finds major differences and subtle
nuances between doctrines does not mean there are
30,000 legitimate versions of the Truth. Divinely inspired,
St. Paul wrote in Ephesians 4:5–6, "One Lord, one faith,
one Baptism; one God and Father of all, who is over all
and through all and in all." We must conclude from this,
and the rest of Scripture, that there is only one true Christian doctrine—that which points to Christ crucified,
raised, and victorious over sin.

As with a builder who lays a solid foundation on solid
ground, the solid Christian faith is "built on the foundation of the apostles and prophets, with Christ Jesus Himself as the chief cornerstone" (Ephesians 2:20). We must be
certain that what we believe, teach, and confess to the
world points only to Christ and His saving work on the
cross.

We who serve the Church as pastors are doubly
accountable before God. If we embrace and then teach
falsehood, we affect far more souls than just ourselves.
Paul tells us that when Christ comes back on the Last Day,
each person's "work will be shown for what it is, because
the Day will bring it to light. It will be revealed with fire,
and the fire will test the quality of each man's work."

This is serious stuff indeed! For our sins, Christ died and rose again. Let us give all thanks to God for His mercy and patience. His Holy Spirit continues to lead us away from false teaching and causes our faith and joy to grow ever stronger. God's Word and sacraments are His divinely appointed building materials for the foundation of our faith in Jesus. With those gifts, God constructs a relationship with us that is built for life everlasting.

Lord Jesus

Keep me in the one true faith by the power of Your Holy Spirit. Help me support the faithful preaching and teaching of Your Holy Word so Your kingdom on earth will continually grow until that great day when You will test every man's worth with fire. I know I will stand on that day because of the blood You shed for me. In Your name. Amen.

Today's Challenge

In prayer, ask the Holy Spirit for help as you resolve to learn even more about God's saving Word. Pray that your pastor will remain faithful to the true Word.

Read Proverbs 7
1 Corinthians 7:1–7

Husbands and Wives: You Belong to One Another

A recent report revealed that the majority of bedroom scenes in movies and television shows involve unmarried men and women. As sure as movies have dialogue, one can expect to see people "expressing their love" in ways reserved strictly for marriage. This information does not surprise us.

It is unfortunate that today's teenagers are growing up in a culture that lies to them about sex and relationships. They are told that sex is no more than recreation and that having sex makes them more mature. The media teach that sex comes before commitment. And many adults in influential positions say they care about youth but encourage condom distribution in public schools, abortion without parental notification, and other trappings of a "sex without consequence" society.

All of the above is justified by the attitude: "Well, kids are going to have sex anyway." With sex viewed as recreation, it is easy to embrace this natural pleasure as free to all—married or unmarried. The pain of sexual abuse, unwanted pregnancy, and immature men who abandon their pregnant girlfriends has become a legacy of society.

That's the bad news. The good news is what God tells us about sex and happiness through the apostle Paul. Paul says that when it comes to true happiness in relationships, husbands and wives must remember they are gifts of God whom He has given to one another. St. Paul wrote:

> But since there is so much immorality, each man should have his own wife, and each woman her own husband. The husband should fulfill his marital duty to his wife, and likewise the wife to her husband. The wife's body does not belong to her alone but also to her husband. In the same way, the husband's body does not belong to him alone but also to his wife. Do not deprive each other except by mutual consent and for a time, so that you may devote yourselves to prayer. Then come together again so that Satan will not tempt you because of your lack of self-control.
>
> *1 Corinthians 7:2–5*

What St. Paul says is loud and clear: Don't "mess" with sex. Like all of God's good and perfect gifts, the devil takes great pleasure in abusing, twisting, and perverting sex until it no longer resembles what God intended it to be. Through Satan's deceit, the world sees sex as a way to find pleasure. Sex then becomes just another way people can exercise their will for their own selfish desires.

God, however, desires for sex to be selfless. Sex is the only human act where a man and woman can completely give of themselves to each other as a profound physical expression of their commitment to join their separate interests and desires into one united life together. When both husband and wife understand sex within the context of God's design, they are able to put the needs and desires of one another before their own. This is the recipe for a long, happy, guilt-free life together in marriage.

Our lives are guilt free because of the saving grace of our Lord, Jesus Christ. No one on earth has ever demonstrated such unselfish love as God's only Son. Christ came to earth as our humble Servant. He lived the perfect life we could not live, then went to the cross to suffer the divine punishment we deserved. Through Baptism, we are united in His death and washed clean so God no longer sees the stain of sin upon us. As we continue to regularly hear God's precious Word and receive the Lord's Supper in worship, our faith in Christ as Savior grows stronger along with renewed understanding of Christ's selfless death for our sake.

Trusting in Jesus alone for our forgiveness involves reflecting God's love in our lives, turning away from sin, and expressing our joy in grateful service to our wife, children, and all whom God has given us. We belong to one another!

Lord Jesus

Through Your selfless love, You put my needs before Your own. Help me, by the power of Your Spirit, to show that same unselfish love toward my wife, children, and all others. In Your holy name. Amen.

Today's Challenge

Do something unselfish for your wife today.

Read Proverbs 5
1 Corinthians 7:10–16

Marriage Lasts a Lifetime

A fair number of people you know may be divorced or may have contemplated divorce at one time or another. Indeed, the society in which we live seems to spend more time focusing on reasons why a person should get out of a marriage that isn't working, than on reasons why couples should reconcile and stay together.

Although we may never be able to turn to society for real help concerning this problem, we are able to turn to God's Word and find His gracious promises to all of us who are married or have been married, regardless of where we are in our marital relationships. Holy Scripture tells us that God intends for marriage to last a lifetime. St. Paul wrote:

> If any brother has a wife who is not a believer and she is willing to live with him, he must not divorce her. And if a woman has a husband who is not a believer and he is willing to live with her, she must not divorce him. For the unbelieving husband has been sanctified through his wife, and the unbelieving wife has been sanctified through her believing husband. ... But if the unbeliever leaves, let him do so. A believing man or woman is not bound in such circumstances; God has called us to live in peace.
>
> *1 Corinthians 7:12–15*

Marriage is often based on a worldly definition of love, a definition of warm and happy feelings. Unfortunately, those warm and happy love feelings tend to diminish with the realities of life. When the passion wanes, the world sees little reason to stay married. If we go around only once, why should we spend the best years of our lives with someone who is not giving us what we need?

Yet the costs incurred as a marriage ends affect more than just husband and wife. Children are left to deal with the death of the family. When either spouse remarries, the children then face the challenge of fitting into a new family while maintaining their identity in their first family.

Although God allows for divorce in two exceptional circumstances (adultery and desertion), it must never be forgotten that God said through His prophet, "Has not the LORD made them one? In flesh and spirit they are His. And why one? Because He was seeking godly offspring. So guard yourself in your spirit, and do not break faith with the wife of your youth. 'I hate divorce,' says the LORD God of Israel" (Malachi 2:15–16).

Paul's inspired words to the people of Corinth reference the point that children belong to their earthly parents as well as to the Lord. A marriage built on the solid foundation of faith in God is well worth the commitment and dedication to diagnose and fix any problem that comes your way.

Well, what if I am divorced right now? The grace of God and the precious blood of God's only Son cover us completely. Although the legal bond of matrimony may be terminated in the eyes of the state, the Christian man knows that divorce cannot destroy the God-given role of the family's man. That means a Christian ex-husband still cares for, prays for, and is ready to assist his ex-wife. As a father, he can make the most of visits, beginning with worship, devotions, and prayer. With God's help, he can strive to be at peace with his former spouse and to meet any and all financial responsibilities. Although a man's role in the life of his family is often severely limited in divorce, that does not mean his love for his family is limited.

Through Holy Baptism, God gives us the faith to trust in the merits of Jesus alone for our salvation. Living in that daily washing by the power of the Holy Spirit through His Word and the Lord's Supper, we also confess our sins to our wives and others we may have offended. That willingness to confess and seek forgiveness is the key God gives through Christ to make marriage last a lifetime!

Lord Jesus

Thank You for the precious gift of marriage. Forgive me for all the times I have taken Your love for granted and for all the times I have taken the love of those around me for granted. Help me by Your Spirit's power to honor the commitments You have entrusted to me. In Your name. Amen.

Today's Challenge

Evaluate how well you are honoring the commitment you made to God and your family. On a sheet of paper, note the things you feel you are doing well and the things you would like to improve. If you like, show this list to a trusted friend and ask for a second opinion.

Love Is What Love Does

Wouldn't it be great if we had a nickel for every time we heard the word *love* in a song on the radio? I think we'd all be millionaires. Love is the universal theme expressed through every art form from painting to sculpture to poetry and so on. There is no end to the lyrics that describe how deep, far, lasting, and strong one person's love is for another. With all of this love going around, why is there so much unloving behavior among people who claim to love one another?

The chief reason for this inconsistency between love talk and love action is that the world's idea of love is basically selfish in nature. A man might woo his lover with emotion-packed words ultimately because he wants something for himself; attention, affection, and physical gratification are just a few possibilities. God has quite a different idea about how love should be expressed between people. Rather than obscure art and flowery words, God requires loving acts. St. Paul wrote:

> Love is patient, love is kind. It does not envy, it does not boast, it is not proud. It is not rude, it is not self-seeking, it is not easily angered, it keeps no record of wrongs. Love does not delight in evil but rejoices with the truth. It always protects, always trusts, always hopes, always perseveres.
>
> *1 Corinthians 13:4–7*

True love, according to God's definition, is not a word that stands all alone; it is always attached to an action or an attribute. Just look at each of the words and attributes St. Paul attached to the word *love:* patient, kind, does not envy, does not boast, is not proud, is not rude, is not self-seeking, is not easily angered, keeps no record of wrongs, does not delight in evil but rejoices in truth, always protects, always trusts, always hopes, and always perseveres. One could hit the top of the charts with a love song using that list.

The last four attributes of love on Paul's list—always protects, always trusts, always hopes, and always perseveres—look to the future. Many marriages fail because a husband and wife are yearning for what used to be. But the couple demonstrating the love Paul describes thanks God for His blessings in their past and anticipates future blessings with great confidence. These blessings include God's guidance and protection in the time the couple has remaining on earth. While children, time to enjoy each other, and the anticipation of a new car, home, and retirement are just a few of the many future blessings that might be desired, these earthly blessings pale in comparison "to the surpassing greatness of knowing Christ Jesus [our] Lord" (Philippians 3:8).

Every one of the love actions listed above was performed perfectly by God's only Son on our behalf. This righteousness of Christ is now ours through faith alone in Him. For all of us who have been baptized into Christ Jesus, our old envious, proud, rude, and self-seeking sinful nature has been crucified with Christ. Having been washed clean in His blood, we know what true love is; it is Christ in us! The Holy Spirit helps us persevere in this life, moving us to forgive one another. The love of God never fails us!

Lord Jesus

You demonstrated Your great love for us by living out each of the actions and attributes of love perfectly. Help me, by the power of Your Holy Spirit, show this same attitude of love to my wife and children. In Your name. Amen.

Today's Challenge

As you listen to the radio today, think about how *love* is described. Is it selfish or unselfish? Then thank God that real love is unselfish, beginning with His love for you in Christ!

Male Sensitivity

What do you think when you hear the phrase "sensitive male"? The phrase makes me smile. After all, historically men have not been known for their sensitivity. As of late, male sensitivity has become a highly prized virtue. Yet at the same time, male insensitivity has almost become a crime.

I don't want my cynicism to give you the wrong idea. Men certainly need to be sensitive and aware of the needs and feelings of those around them. Yet society's definition of *sensitivity* seems to be much more nebulous. The world's version of sensitivity seems to equate becoming insensitive to everything except that which you want or need. Sound confusing?

For those confused or frustrated by the world's definition of sensitivity, the Bible provides much-needed guidance. St. Paul wrote:

> So I tell you this, and insist on it in the Lord, that you must no longer live as the Gentiles do, in the futility of their thinking. They are darkened in their understanding and separated from the life of God because of the ignorance that is in them due to the hardening of their hearts. Having lost all sensitivity, they have given themselves over to sensuality so as to indulge in every kind of impurity, with a continual lust for more.
>
> *Ephesians 4:17–19*

In 2 Corinthians 11:14–15, Paul says, "Satan himself masquerades as an angel of light. It is not surprising, then, if his servants masquerade as servants of righteousness. Their end will be what their actions deserve."

All people have a very basic sense of right and wrong because God has written His Law on their hearts. However, sinful humans manipulate this sense of right and wrong, redefining the terms to suit their own sinful appetites. For example, say a man pours massive amounts of time, money, and energy into campaigns to save the whales and the rainforests. Yet he also fights equally hard to uphold the law that defends a mother's right to abort her own child.

This is how the devil operates. He distorts our perceptions while covertly drawing us further into his web of sin and death. We allow our contemporaries to convince us that our actions are just and righteous without ever measuring those actions against God's Word.

Compare what God calls "losing sensitivity" with what the world calls "insensitive:" "Having lost all sensitivity, they have given themselves over to sensuality so as to indulge in every kind of impurity, with a continual lust for more."

True sensitivity in God's eyes includes being particularly tuned to what God desires for us in His Holy Word. Ephesians chapter four says, "You however, did not come to know Christ that way. Surely you heard of Him and were taught in Him in accordance with the truth that is in Jesus. You were taught, with regard to your former way of life, to put off your old self, which is being corrupted by its deceitful desires; to be made new in the attitude of your minds; and to put on the new self, created to be like God in true righteousness and holiness" (Ephesians 4:20–24).

This sensitivity is part of the wonderful gift the Holy Spirit put into our hearts at Baptism. God's kind of sensitivity exhibits itself in a heart that beats for God in true faith and love, and in caring love for others. This sensitivity was first shown to us in God's Son, Jesus, who came as our Servant to hold sin and death captive. Jesus showed us the ultimate sensitivity when He overcame the terror of death and the grave with the guarantee of our own bodily resurrection to eternal life on the Last Day.

Thank God that He has made you His own and given you His sensitivity in Christ.

Lord Jesus

Keep me sensitive to Your desires for me as expressed in Your saving Word, that I may be truly sensitive to my family and to all whom You have placed in my life. In Your name. Amen.

Today's Challenge

Show the world that you are a biblically sensitive male.

Read Proverbs 10:1–14
Ephesians 5:1–21

Spare Yourself a Lot of Trouble

When you think back to your high school days, you can probably recall people who were always in trouble with their parents, teachers, or even law enforcement. On the other hand, you can probably think of others who were never in very serious trouble or perhaps they were not in any trouble at all. Which of these camps did you fit into most during high school?

Today's reading from Scripture shows us something very important about our God. Although He demands that we be as perfect as He is under His Law, He also loves us with a compassionate love, conscious of the troubling hurt we experience through sin. Out of His compassionate love, He sent the crucified and risen Lord. Living as forgiven children of the loving God, Paul exhorts us to be filled with the Spirit so we might live to glorify God through fruitful lives rather than sinking more deeply into the troublesome darkness of sin. St. Paul wrote:

> Be very careful, then, how you live—not as unwise but as wise, making the most of every opportunity, because the days are evil. Therefore do not be foolish, but understand what the Lord's will is. Do not get drunk on wine, which leads to debauchery. Instead, be filled with the Spirit. ... Submit to one another out of reverence for Christ.
>
> *Ephesians 5:15–21*

Let's take a closer look at verses 15–21:

Making the most of every opportunity. Seeing each day as truly filled with opportunities transforms our entire outlook on life. Our Lord balances our joys and sorrows, strengthens our faith, and develops our character and perseverance as His own beloved children. Whereas the unbeliever raises an angry fist to heaven in times of trouble, we lift our eyes to the Lord on bad days as well as good. In the strength He provides, we seek to praise Him in every opportunity.

Seek to understand the Lord's will. Only as we faithfully worship, feeding on His Word and sacraments, can we be brought closer to God and begin to see how God works His will in our lives.

Be filled with the Spirit. Since sin and the Holy Spirit are incompatible, only one can be our master. As we grab hold of the faith that is ours in Christ, the Holy Spirit continues to strengthen our faith and turn us away from sin.

Speak to one another with psalms, hymns, and spiritual songs. God calls us to express our faith outwardly through kind and encouraging words to one another. As we come together each day and weekly in worship, let us raise our voices together in praise to the Lord.

Sing and make music in your heart to the Lord. Even when you aren't speaking aloud or singing with others, you can praise the Lord with love and thanksgiving in your heart.

Always giving thanks to God the Father for everything, in the name of our Lord Jesus Christ. It is Jesus who suffered the punishment we deserved. By our Lord's resurrection, we know for certain that God has accepted His Son's sacrifice on our behalf. This gift of salvation through faith gives us the freedom to live totally for God in service to Him—free from the fear of guilt and condemnation.

Submit to one another out of reverence for Christ. Our freedom from guilt and condemnation allows us to submit to others. Our trusting the self-sacrificing love of our Savior is reflected in our actions, of submitting in love toward our wives, children, and the world.

Lord Jesus

I know I am prone to getting into trouble. I often fall short of what You expect from a Christian husband and father. Please forgive me. By Your Holy Spirit, fill me with gratitude and strength so I will both desire and accomplish the things You want me to do to Your great honor and glory. In Your name. Amen.

Today's Challenge

Consider your daily schedule. What opportunities do you have to bring honor and glory to Christ? Is it refusing to join in water cooler gossip? Or can you invite a co-worker to church? Ask the Lord for His support and guidance as you set out to share His love and forgiveness at every opportunity.

LIKE A WELL-OILED MACHINE

One of the duties I perform as a volunteer firefighter is the regular inspection of equipment used for the job. I check air tanks, masks, and the "jaws of life," for example. One of the most important things on the equipment checklist is to start every engine and check all fluids to make sure they are at the proper level. Oil is the lifeblood of a machine. Without oil, an ingeniously designed piece of equipment becomes as useful as a paperweight.

In recent years, the lines between male and female have become blurred. The unique roles God has given to each are often ignored and replaced with selfishness. In turn, these selfish motivations blur the lines that could potentially connect the two. As a result, too many marriages have run dry—like a machine that has lost its oil plug.

God has provided the oil of faith for family relationships—faith in Christ as Savior and Lord. This is a faith that expresses itself in mutual respect and love shown by unselfish service. Read what St. Paul said in Ephesians chapter five:

> Submit to one another out of reverence for Christ. ... In this same way, husbands ought to love their wives as their own bodies. He who loves his wife loves himself. After all, no one ever hated his own body, but he feeds and cares for it, just as Christ does the church—for we are members of His body.
>
> *Ephesians 5:21–30*

In today's society, love has become almost inter-changeable with the self-gratifying act of sex. God's love, on the other hand, puts the needs of a spouse ahead of one's own. Although candy and flowers or other gifts are wonderful gestures, Christ-like love is demonstrated when a husband jumps out of bed at 2:00 A.M. to help his wife clean up the bed of their sick child.

Think of your wife as a gracious gift from God, and put her and your family's needs ahead of your own. As you respect and honor her God-given role, she too will respect and honor your God-given role as head of the family. The family will be strengthened and your children will experi-ence Christ's love as reflected through the relationship you and your wife share. Unselfish mutual love and respect are precious gifts from God—perhaps rare in many marriages today.

The source of this unselfish love is Jesus who unselfish-ly loved us. Jesus loved us so much that He became our Servant and our Brother. He suffered God's anger on the cross and was punished in our place to bring us salvation and eternal life. As the Holy Spirit plants Christ's love in our hearts, He gives us the strength to love our wives and children as He desires. With Christ as the source, the oil in our machines will never run dry.

Gracious Lord

Give me strength to fight the temptation of selfish-ness. Remind me that You put all of my needs ahead of Your own when You came to redeem my soul from death. With gratitude in my heart, I eagerly desire to please You by serving my family and putting their needs ahead of my own. In Jesus' precious name. Amen.

Today's Challenge

Think about things that are important to your wife and your children. Commit to doing some of these activities in gratitude for what Christ has done for you.

Read Proverbs 21:4–24
Philippians 2:1–11

Humility: The Antidote for Arguments

Consider the heated debates, little or big, you have had with your wife: Did you both want different things? Did she dig in her heels as much as you did? How did she express her feelings and how did you express yours? What was her tone of voice and what was yours? Were you sensitive to her needs or were you more sensitive to your own? At the moment of the argument, what was more important: what she wanted or what you wanted?

If you really enjoy arguing with your wife, you are not going to like what I have to say. If, however, you want to avoid unproductive contests, pay attention to what God has said through His apostle Paul. God tells us that humility is the true antidote for arguments. St. Paul wrote:

> If you have any encouragement from being united with Christ, if any comfort from His love, if any fellowship with the Spirit, if any tenderness and compassion, then make my joy complete by being like-minded, having the same love, being one in spirit and purpose. Do nothing out of selfish ambition or vain conceit, but in humility consider others better than yourselves. Each of you should look not only to your own interests, but also to the interests of others.
>
> *Philippians 2:1–4*

The opening questions in this devotion have the common thread of self-defense. Surely you know the feeling. Your wife may level a perfectly valid question at you concerning something you did or did not do, and it cuts right to the core. The heat of anger wells up from your toes and sets fire to every nerve like an out-of-control blaze. It won't be extinguished until you express it in the most cleverly crafted sentence that both defends your action and puts her in her place.

Now let's pretend Jesus came to earth to "put us in our place"—to give us what we truly deserved. What would we receive? If the world even continued to exist, we would be facing a hopeless death with an eternity of hell to follow. That would be getting what we deserve!

Thank God Jesus didn't share our sinful, selfish attitude. Philippians says, "Your attitude should be the same as that of Christ Jesus: Who, being in very nature God, did not consider equality with God something to be grasped, but made Himself nothing, taking the very nature of a servant, being made in human likeness. And being found in appearances as a man, He humbled Himself and became obedient to death—even death on a cross!" (Philippians 2:5–8).

Can anyone imagine Jesus running around with an attitude saying, "Hey you! Watch this! (performs a miracle) See! I'm God!"? Of course not! Everything we know about our Lord proves exactly the opposite really happened. Jesus humbled Himself for our sake. His agony and death on the cross was the only perfect way God could keep sin, death, and the power of the devil captive forever.

My dear friends, you and I are nothing more than complex piles of dust and ash. Our Creator was pleased to humble Himself for our sakes and become our Servant to save us. How can we, then, be so preoccupied with ourselves that self-defense reigns supreme over Christ's desire that we follow His example and humble ourselves before others? Grounded in faith, Christ enables us to follow in His footsteps as husbands, fathers, sons, neighbors, employers, employees, friends, and in whatever other roles we occupy in this life. St. Paul writes, "In humility consider others better than yourselves. Each of you should look not only to your own interests, but also to the interests of others."

As the Holy Spirit works in our hearts, this Christ-like humility becomes genuine and deepens throughout our life. We may even discover that humility indeed is the antidote for arguments.

Lord Jesus

Please forgive me for every time I have hurt my wife with unkind words. Give me strength to follow your example and always humble myself to her, my children, and all others as better than myself so I may cherish, protect, and serve them with all my heart by the power of Your Holy Spirit. In Your name. Amen.

Today's Challenge

Next time you feel a heated debate coming on, ask your wife if the two of you can continue the discussion a little later. A short break and a prayer asking God to change your heart will serve to clear your mind and get you back on track with a more caring and loving attitude.

You're a Star

Every spring the eyes of the media turn to Hollywood to see which of the brightest stars will win the coveted Oscar. We are used to associating the word *star* with movie and television celebrities. But how did the word *star* become associated with big-time actors and actresses? The answer likely lies with a star's ability to shine. Just as celestial stars shine in the night, these performers shine with worldly glitz and earthly glamour on the silver screen.

Today's portion of Scripture tells us that we have just as much claim to stardom as media celebrity. Paul's letter to the Philippians shows that God has made us His stars in the world as we trust in Jesus as Savior and live as faithful husbands and fathers. St. Paul wrote:

> Do everything without complaining or arguing, so that you may become blameless and pure, children of God without fault in a crooked and depraved generation, in which you shine like stars in the universe as you hold out the Word of Life—in order that I may boast on the day of Christ that I did not run or labor for nothing.
>
> *Philippians 2:14–16*

Refusing to argue, like refusing to complain, speaks volumes against actually engaging in vocal combat. This does not mean you are licensed to use silence as a weapon. Smug silence does not befit a child of God who walks in the humility of Jesus Christ. Rather, refusing to argue or complain is the difference between knowing when to

167

speak and knowing when speaking will further aggravate the situation.

Fire requires three things to burn: oxygen, fuel, and a heat source. Remove any of these and the fire goes out. If another person tries to draw us into a confrontation, the fight will snuff itself out if we refrain from returning angry words, looks, or actions. God uses our restraint to distinguish us as His children, to shine like stars.

God wants very much for us to stand out from the crowd and to shine like stars in a sin-darkened world. Because God no longer sees our sin for Jesus' sake, we have every reason to rejoice as Paul encouraged. This gift of eternal life is our motivation to turn away from sin and live blameless and pure lives as "children of God without fault in a crooked and depraved generation."

Clearly God means that His stars are human points of light that reflect the glory of Jesus in a world that doesn't have a clue about God's saving love. Husbands and fathers have a lifetime of opportunities to shine like stars. A man who understands and demonstrates the importance of Christ in his home will guide His family, by the power of the Holy Spirit, to become God's special stars too!

Lord Jesus

In the darkness of this sinful world, You are my Light. As the moon reflects the light of the sun, make me reflect Your radiance through what I say and do. Then I will shine like Your star to the glory of Your great name. In Your gracious name. Amen.

Today's Challenge

Next time you see a movie star, consider whose light this star is reflecting—the world's or Christ's?

Read Proverbs 15:16–33
1 Timothy 6:3–6

The Root of All Evil

After you read the title above, you may have thought, *Money is the root of all evil.* Contrary to popular belief, money is not the root of all evil. Like so many familiar passages of Scripture, this verse is often used out of context. It is the *love* of money that is the root of all evil. In fact, the root of any evil is the love, trust, and fear of anything over and above God.

Although today's title might sound foreboding, today's message is really about the key to lasting happiness. As we turn to St. Paul's encouraging letter to the young Pastor Timothy, we find sound counsel for our own priorities. The apostle wrote:

> For the love of money is a root of all kinds of evil. ... But you, man of God, flee from all this, and pursue righteousness, godliness, faith, love, endurance and gentleness. Fight the good fight of the faith.
>
> *1 Timothy 6:10–12*

Isn't it amazing how things our parents never had are now viewed as indispensable by us? As I write these devotions, I cannot imagine doing them without my computer. Photocopiers, e-mail and the Internet, VCRs and DVDs, CDs, cell phones, pagers, and Global Positioning Systems are just a sampling of the vast world of the once-unimaginable conveniences, gadgets, and tools accessible today. How easy it is to let the lack of some or many of these modern amenities lead to unhappiness!

St. Paul may not have had a laptop, flip phone, or GPS, but what he told Timothy is just as relevant today as it was then. Money and all the worldly goods it can buy are morally neutral. Aside from goods and services that foster immorality and other kinds of sin, the products and services that make our lives easier are okay with God, and can even be considered gifts from Him.

However, the money that acquires these high-tech necessities should never become the source of our happiness. Sinful desire can easily turn the gift of money into a false god when wealth tempts us to believe we don't need God's help in sustaining our lives. Paul describes how this process works, "People who want to get rich fall into temptation and a trap and into many foolish and harmful desires that plunge men into ruin and destruction" (1 Timothy 6:9).

Placing these things above God leads us to destruction. But thanks be to God that He leads us to godly happiness. Paul said, "But godliness with contentment is great gain. For we brought nothing into the world, and we can take nothing out of it. But if we have food and clothing, we will be content with that" (1 Timothy 6:6–8).

The greatest necessity God has provided for us is our redemption from sin—every sin that leads us to destruction. The gift of forgiveness and eternal life has been purchased with an asset so valuable it lies beyond human comprehension: the precious blood of God's only Son. Because of sin, we cannot fully comprehend the depth of God's love. So He sent Jesus to show us that by dying on the cross, He has paid for our sins in full. Through the power of the Holy Spirit, we trust that the deed to our home in heaven is signed, sealed, and delivered to us in our Baptism.

Through the power of the Holy Spirit, we strive to place God first in our lives so nothing can keep us, our wives, and our children from weekly worship and the celebration of God's undeserved love for us in Christ. He will help us avoid stumbling over the many roots of evil.

Lord Jesus

It is very easy to find myself chasing after material things. Forgive me and fill me with gratitude each day for the greatest gift You have given me, the gift of eternal life. Help me be content with Your good gifts whether I have a lot or a little, because in You I am always rich. In Your name. Amen.

Today's Challenge

Place a slip of paper with a cross on it in your checkbook to remind you that you and your family have been redeemed by Christ crucified, and that you hold the deed to one awesome home in heaven.

Read Psalm 1
James 1:1–18

—>●<—

No Pain—No Gain

When I was in high school, the weight room had a sign on the wall that read, "No Pain—No Gain." Although my commitment to weight resistance training ended the day after it started, I understood that sign on the wall. Unless you made your body hurt, there would be no gain of increased muscle strength.

There is a form of spiritual training children of God must also endure. This training causes pain that leads to an eternal gain. In his epistle, St. James said:

> Consider it pure joy, my brothers, whenever you face trials of many kinds, because you know that the testing of your faith develops perseverance. Perseverance must finish its work so that you may be mature and complete, not lacking anything.
>
> *James 1:2–4*

There are days when the weight lifter dreads going through his routine because he knows how much it is going to hurt. But he does it anyway because he trusts the pain is necessary to reach his goal. Similarly, we face trials and hardships that come from those resisting a God and those who believe in Him. Some days we may dread answering those who constantly challenge our faith. Often we'd rather let mean or derogatory comments slip by than confront the problem and exercise our faith. Despite fatigue and silent fears, the trusting Christian prays for strength, confident that God works through him in the face of challenges and persecution.

Being a husband and father are the two greatest responsibilities a man can have. Nothing can compare to the joy a warm and loving wife brings to a husband's life, just as nothing can compare to the wonderful feeling the love of his children brings to a father. Still, there are days when nothing seems to go right. Whether grief or hostility come from loved ones, coworkers, friends, or strangers, we simply cannot quit the responsibility of being a faithful and loving coworker, neighbor, friend, husband, and father. We must press on, focused on the goal of righteousness Jesus set before us through His death and resurrection.

Thankfully, God sent His only Son, our Lord Jesus Christ, to become perfectly familiar with our grief and pain. By His perfect life under the Law, Jesus took our place and put an end to the Law's threat of eternal punishment through His innocent suffering and death on the cross. Our Savior's bodily resurrection on Easter morning promises that we too will rise again with perfect bodies when Jesus comes back to take us home.

God has set the goal before us, but unlike the weight lifter, who grows stronger only by his own efforts, God increases our trust by the power of the Holy Spirit.

While physical pain awaits us as we struggle through the hardships and trials of being God's disciple, God draws us ever closer to Him through worship, Word, and Sacrament. The strength of faith that follows is a wonderful gain for the whole family!

Dearest Jesus

Thank You for using my good days to encourage me to do what You want me to do. Thank You for using my difficult days to develop perseverance and the wisdom I need to remain faithful as Your child, as a husband, and as a father. In Your holy name. Amen.

Today's Challenge

Identify just one event or circumstance in your life that, at the present moment, you consider a pain. Ask God for His wisdom and to help you turn this pain into a God-glorifying gain.

Read Proverbs 15:1–15
James 3:1–12

Watch Your Tongue

Throughout these devotions, I have tried to come up with illustrations that clarify the message from God's Word. Today, however, I surrender! The selected portion of Holy Scripture from St. James is so full of beautiful illustrations that to add another would only take away from the thought itself. Instead, I would like to devote the extra space to the entire message from today's reading. As you read, keep today's theme in mind, "Watch your tongue!" James the brother of Jesus wrote:

Not many of you should presume to be teachers, my brothers, because you know that we who teach will be judged more strictly. We all stumble in many ways. If anyone is never at fault in what he says, he is a perfect man, able to keep his whole body in check. When we put bits into the mouths of horses to make them obey us, we can turn the whole animal. Or take ships as an example. Although they are so large and are driven by strong winds, they are steered by a very small rudder wherever the pilot wants to go. Likewise the tongue is a small part of the body, but it makes great boasts. Consider what a great forest is set on fire by a small spark. The tongue also is a fire, a world of evil among the parts of the body. It corrupts the whole person, sets the whole course of his life on fire, and is itself set on fire by hell. All kinds of animals, birds, reptiles and creatures of the sea are being tamed and have been tamed by man, but no man can tame the tongue. It is a restless evil, full of deadly poison. With the tongue we praise our Lord and Father, and with it we curse men, who have been made in God's likeness. Out of the same mouth come praise and cursing. My brothers, this should not be. Can both fresh water and salt water flow from the same spring? My brothers, can a fig tree bear olives, or a grapevine bear figs? Neither can a salt spring produce fresh water.

James 3:1–12

James, the biological half brother of our Lord Jesus Christ, is thought to be the author of this book. At first, James and his other brothers did not believe that Jesus, their biological brother, was also their Creator and Redeemer (a hard pill to swallow, indeed). Later he believed and became very prominent in the church of Jerusalem.

The audience to whom James directed his writing was mostly made up of established Christians. While they trusted that salvation came by God's grace alone through faith in Jesus Christ. The devil was at work, causing problems in the lives of the Christians and the Church as a whole. In this particular passage, James specifically refers to sins of the tongue. His message remains relevant today.

How many times has your tongue caused grief? A heated argument breaks out between you and your wife, and past sins—long forgiven, but not forgotten—get dragged up and reintroduced as if they had just occurred. As sinners, we fall into the trap. As redeemed children of God, we are called to a different type of behavior. We are called to follow the example of Jesus.

Jesus watched His tongue. Even when He spoke forcefully, He spoke out of perfect, divine anger at men who were responsible for leading God's people away from His Word. It was those same people who mounted a kangaroo court determined to kill Jesus. These men—the Pharisees, ruling priests, and other teachers of the Law—did not watch their tongues. They mocked Jesus, blaspheming the very God who allowed Himself to be abused, tortured, and crucified to satisfy the just anger of God toward all sinners. Yet Jesus, the sacrificial Lamb, stayed silent.

A great deal of hurt is heaped upon others through inappropriate and harmful words. Some husbands may continue to live with foot-in-mouth syndrome for the rest of their lives. But Jesus has taken even these sins to the cross. Through the daily washing of our sins in Christ, we trust that God will work in us the ability to tame our tongues.

Lord Jesus

It is frightening how easily harmful words pour out of my mouth when I am angry. Forgive me and have mercy on me! Help me to speak, think, and act in ways that are pleasing to You. By the power of Your Holy Spirit, give me the strength to restrain my tongue, harnessing it so I bring only glory to Your name by what I say. In Your name. Amen.

Today's Challenge

Identify times and situations when you are most likely to sin with your tongue. Bookmark those times in your mind, so you can be prepared with a prayer when they arise.

It's a Dog-Eat-Dog World ...
So Don't Be a Dog

In the movie *Wall Street,* the character played by Michael Douglas said "Greed is good." That movie reflected the media's attempt to label the 1980s "the decade of greed." But surely the 1990s gave the '80s a run for their money.

In truth, greed has belonged to all decades since the beginning of time as a sinful condition of the human heart. The phrase "dog-eat-dog" that made its debut long before the 1980s, refers to the attitude that all is fair as long as you get what you're going after. Today, amidst the trials of our dog-eat-dog world, the Lord calls us to *not* be dogs. In the following passage, St. James continues to give advice for godly living, providing a much different way for God's children to look at life:

> Who is wise and understanding among you? Let him show it by his good life, by deeds done in the humility that comes from wisdom. But if you harbor bitter envy and selfish ambition in your hearts, do not boast about it or deny the truth. Such "wisdom" does not come down from heaven but is earthly, unspiritual, of the devil. For where you have envy and selfish ambition, there you find disorder and every evil practice.
>
> *James 3:13–16*

If we were to ask mature adults if they thought they were good people, we could expect them to say yes. The problem is that most people are blind to how sinful they really are. Sinful humans cannot handle this truth because their hearts, by nature, are filled with sinful thoughts and tendencies, such as "bitter envy and selfish ambition."

Unbelieving people might try their best to conceal their sins and wickedness in words and actions while trying to take advantage of others in dog-eat-dog fashion. But God searches every person's heart and knows the truth. Through James, He urges us to guard against such "wisdom" that comes from any source other than Him.

God reveals to us His true wisdom, "the wisdom that comes from heaven." The Son of God came down from heaven and became man in the womb of the Virgin Mary. He lived a perfect life for us, offered Himself on the cross as the one perfect sacrifice for the sins of the whole world. To trust Jesus Christ as our Savior from sin is to be truly wise in God's sight.

Children of God express their gratitude for this gift of salvation by living according to the power of the Holy Spirit, leading them to live wisely "by deeds done in the humility that comes from wisdom." James said, "The wisdom that comes from heaven is first of all pure; then peace-loving, considerate, submissive, full of mercy and good fruit, impartial and sincere. Peacemakers who sow in peace raise a harvest of righteousness" (James 3:17–18).

Dogs in a dog-eat-dog world place their own greed and ambition over the needs of others. But the wisdom of God, lived out in humility, is a reflection of Christ in you.

Heavenly Father

You have created me and redeemed me from sin. Let me reflect Your love as a humble and obedient child. Give me the desire to serve others for their benefit instead of for my own. In Jesus' name. Amen.

Today's Challenge

Make an effort to know more the families of your coworkers (at least enough to ask how they are doing). Every day, bring a different associate and his or her family to God in prayer with special requests for their particular needs.

Choose Your Friends Carefully and Love Them

What thoughts come to mind when you hear the word *popularity?* It depends on how old you are, doesn't it? What did popularity mean when you were in junior high or high school? Popularity was, and still is, a much sought-after status for many teenagers. The popular kids are those who are well-liked, respected, and generally spared the teasing and exclusion often endured by the unpopular. If we had been asked as teenagers to predict the future for the popular kids, we would probably have assumed that they would marry the best-looking people, have the best-looking kids, get the most prestigious jobs, and remain the most popular in their adult years.

There is one flaw in these assumptions. Popularity often comes at a price. To stay popular, a person may become a slave to popular things—the "right" clothes, the "right" music, and the "right" friends. Ben Franklin said, "A friend in need is a friend indeed." Sometimes popular friends aren't friends at all. Maybe they are just using others to stroke their own egos. Or perhaps they are people who won't hang in there half as long as they are willing to hang out.

In today's lesson, James points out that wise Christians choose their friends carefully, then treat them with love. James wrote:

> You adulterous people, don't you know that friendship

with the world is hatred toward God? Anyone who chooses to be a friend of the world becomes an enemy of God. Or do you think Scripture says without reason that the spirit He caused to live in us envies intensely? But He gives us more grace. ... Submit yourselves, then, to God. Resist the devil, and he will flee from you. Come near to God and He will come near to you.

James 4:4–8

It hurts when we feel we aren't liked very much. We can easily become jealous or envious of those who enjoy popularity—at any age. The desire to be liked is a powerful force to contend with in our lives. In an attempt to be liked, many will sacrifice what they know is God pleasing on the altar of popularity. As adults, the quest for being liked may result in unscrupulous business practices for the "good" of the team, joining in gossip, or bragging about sins to fit in with the rest of the guys.

Striving after this kind of friendship with the world is deadly—eternally deadly. James uses the shocking word *adulterous* to describe anyone who prizes worldly popularity and friendship more than being a child of God. Adultery has its roots in the Old Testament. God described His relationship with His people Israel as that of a loving, faithful husband to his wife. When Israel turned away from the Lord to worship false gods, God described Israel as going after other lovers. God still desires to share that intimate bond with His people, especially since He has made the bond perfect through His only Son, our Lord Jesus Christ.

God gave Himself completely to us when His precious Son came to our earth and saved us from "false friends" who only wanted to take something away from us. These good-for-nothing "friends" are the devil, this sinful world, and even our own sinful flesh. Since we are so weak, Jesus came to destroy our alliances with the devil by His suffering and death for us on the cross.

Through our Baptism, we have died to the world and its power over our lives, and have been raised again with Jesus as eternal friends with God. Knowing the debt we owe God for His undeserved love for us in Christ, the Holy Spirit moves our hearts to grateful humility.

With your wife and children by your side, you have the joy of being drawn closer to God through regular worship as He reveals Himself through His Word, the waters of Baptism, and the bread and wine of Holy Communion. Strengthened in faith, you are enabled to resist the attempts of Satan to seduce you, and rest in the grace of His forgiveness until you rest in His loving arms forever in heaven. God is our Friend in need, and our best Friend indeed!

Lord Jesus

Give me each day the wisdom of Your Holy Spirit that I might appreciate ever more all good gifts from You. Help me to never take any of these gifts for granted, and to daily stay close to Your Word. Through Your Spirit's power, may I be drawn closer to You. In Your name. Amen.

Today's Challenge

Consider who you would name as your closest and dearest friends. Drop them an e-mail or note expressing your gratitude to God for their friendship.

Why Do You Love Me?

How many young ladies have lost their virginity to imma-ture men who have used the line, "If you love me, you will …"? As you know, that is not love. That is selfish deceitful lust. Real love is a wonderful gift from God. The ability of a man to love a woman and vice versa is God's work in us. All of us have told our wives we love them, but what would you do if your wife responded by asking, *"Why* do you love me?" What would you tell her? Today the apos-tle John gives us the most important reason why we love our wives. St. John wrote:

> Dear friends, let us love one another, for love comes from God. Everyone who loves has been born of God and knows God. Whoever does not love does not know God, because God is love. This is how God showed His love among us: He sent His one and only Son into the world that we might live through Him. … No one has ever seen God; but if we love one another, God lives in us and His love is made complete in us.
>
> *1 John 4:7–12*

Truly loving one another is a work of God upon the human heart. The Bible tells us that genuine love comes from God alone! John wrote, "This is love: not that we loved God, but that He loved us and sent His Son as an atoning sacrifice for our sins. Dear friends, since God so loved us, we also ought to love one another" (1 John 4: 10–11).

God's Son, our Lord Jesus Christ, is both the way to eternal life and the perfect model for the kind of love God wants us to show one another. By nature we are sinful—blind, spiritually dead, and enemies of God. How then can we ever be capable of loving others the way God wants us to? The answer is in God's love for us through Jesus.

Out of great love for us, God sent His only Son to die for our sins. Through the Holy Spirit, God's love takes root in our hearts and overflows to others. Without faith in Christ, real love is impossible.

When sinners ask God "How much do You love me?", the answer lies outside the city walls of Jerusalem where God's Son suffered mockery, contempt, and torture for our sake. Christ took upon Himself every ounce of the Father's anger against all sin until the full punishment was satisfied. That's how much God loves us—that He would sacrifice His only Son for the forgiveness of our sins.

The love of God through Christ was poured out into your heart the day you were baptized. If you became a child of God after infancy, then faith came through the hearing of the Good News of Jesus Christ. Either way, the Holy Spirit is responsible for bringing the saving shaft of light into your sin-darkened heart and revealing Christ as the only Son of the only true God. In the same manner, the Holy Spirit empowers you to shine with the light of Christ's love to your wife and children.

As you daily and weekly read, listen to, and meditate upon His Word, the Holy Spirit continues to perform His miraculous work in your heart and in the hearts of your wife and children. John wrote, "Since God so loved us, we also ought to love one another. No one has ever seen God; but if we love one another, God lives in us and His love is made complete in us" (1 John 4:11–12).

When you lead your family to the loving arms of Jesus, worshiping together and expressing your unselfish love and concern for their welfare, you demonstrate *why* you really love them—for Christ's sake!

Lord Jesus

Thank You for teaching me what it means to love. You sacrificed Yourself for me through Your innocent suffering and death so I might live with You forever. Help me show that same unselfish kind of love toward everyone, beginning with my wife and children. In Your name. Amen.

Today's Challenge

Tell your wife why you love her, even if she hasn't asked.

Part III:

The Father for the Family

Read Psalm 26
Genesis 6–8

IN THE FATHER'S WAKE

Here is a story my dad told about a fishing trip his church's men's club took 30 years ago:

"We were up north in the Superior National Forest, having just portaged our boats on a flatbed truck from Lake Vermilion to Trout Lake. Trout Lake was the last lake in the chain that allowed power boats. As we got into our boats, the driver of the lead boat told my friend (the driver of my boat) to 'stay in my wake and never leave it.'

"As we started up the lake, my friend pulled out of the wake and began to run alongside the lead boat. Immediately, the lead boat's driver cut his engine and said 'When I said, "Stay in my wake," I meant it! Look!'

"Only a few yards away, in the middle of the lake, we saw water splashing over table rock that was hidden only a few inches beneath the water. Had we left the wake of the lead boat and ventured where we *thought* it was safe, we surely would have broken our fiberglass boat to bits. Needless to say, my friend never left the wake of the leader after that."

The elements of this true "fish story"—the water, the rock, the safety of the leader's wake—are too irresistible for a pastor to pass up. You could probably take these elements and construct your own application, but permit me to apply this story to the special relationship a father has with his child. As we consider today's lesson based on the account of Noah and the flood, we see the timeless necessity of remaining within the wake of a faithful father. Moses wrote:

> The LORD saw how great man's wickedness on the earth had become, and that every inclination of the thoughts of his heart was only evil all the time. The LORD was grieved that He had made man on the earth, and His heart was filled with pain. So the LORD said, "I will wipe mankind, whom I have created, from the face of the earth—men and animals, and creatures that move along the ground, and birds of the air—for I am grieved that I have made them." But Noah found favor in the eyes of the LORD.
>
> *Genesis 6:5–8*

In the opening words of today's lesson, we see that God is grieved over the sins of humankind. The people He created had left His wake, loving worldly things above God and refusing to love one another. The world was corrupt and in sin, and God resolved to destroy it in punishment.

Yet God saw that Noah still knew and trusted in the Lord as God. For the sake of Noah and his family, God destroyed the earth in such a way that those who believed in Him were saved. The waters that brought God's judgment were also the waters that saved. Today, through the waters of Baptism, the Holy Spirit brings God's grace and salvation to us. St. Peter wrote, "In [the ark] only a few people, eight in all, were saved through water, and this water symbolizes Baptism that now saves you also—not the removal of dirt from the body but the pledge of a good conscience toward God. It saves you by the resurrection of Jesus Christ" (1 Peter 3:20–21).

Holy Baptism doesn't symbolize God's grace. Holy Baptism is a means through which His grace is actually poured out on you and faith is created in your heart. The real, historic event of the Flood is a *symbol* of the salvation given to us in our Baptism.

By creating faith in Jesus alone for their salvation, the Holy Spirit inspires men to make a wake in which wives and children can find safety and comfort for their own faith in Christ to grow. By trusting in the Captain of our salvation, all God's people can live with the joyful reassurance they will arrive safely in God's everlasting harbor of heaven.

Heavenly Father

Thank You for the gift of Your saving grace poured over me through the waters of Baptism. By the power of Your Spirit, help me to stay in the wake of Your love and mercy. Lead my wife and children to follow along through the dangers of this life. In Jesus' name. Amen.

Today's Challenge

Take your child(ren) fishing. If you have a boat, point out the wake made by the boat and tell them about today's lesson. Listen to your own Father, in Jesus' name.

THE MOVE

How many of us have taken a promotion or transfer to a completely different region in the country with its own distinct culture? If you have ever pulled up stakes, you know the stress involved. In fact, making such a move can be downright scary. Unfamiliar situations—no matter how many good opportunities they present—create unwelcome anxieties. But God's promise to be with us always helps us cope with the enormous stress of moving.

Today we are introduced to a man whom God made the father of a great nation. God asked a lot of Abraham and in faith Abraham obeyed. Moses records:

> The LORD had said to Abram, "Leave your country, your people and your father's household and go to the land I will show you. I will make you into a great nation and I will bless you; I will make your name great, and you will be a blessing. I will bless those who bless you, and whoever curses you I will curse; and all peoples on earth will be blessed through you." So Abram left, as the LORD had told him; and Lot went with him. Abram was seventy-five years old when he set out from Haran.
>
> *Genesis 12:1–4*

Seventy-five years old! Hardly the age for a career change. While you and I plan to enjoy a little time off before the Lord calls us home, the Lord called Abraham to start a home for God's people that would eventually become the nation of Israel. "By faith Abraham when called to go to a place he would later receive as his inheritance, obeyed and went" (Hebrews 11:8). "By faith ... Abraham was enabled to become a father because [God] considered him faithful" (Hebrews 11:11). Abraham's faith expressed itself in obedience and confidence in God's trustworthiness.

We also live by faith, trusting in God and His love for us. All who trust in Jesus as their Savior are members of Abraham's spiritual family who follow in His footsteps of acting on the basis of God's promises. Like Abraham, we do not call this earth our real home; we are truly pilgrims in this life. We have been set free from worldly concerns and tribulations by the precious blood of Christ. Jesus died on the cross to pay the debt of our sin so we will live in our heavenly home with God forever. For Jesus' sake, we received our eternal inheritance when we were baptized.

We remain in Abraham's faithful family as we continue to attend worship with our family, hear God's Word, and receive the Lord's Supper. Through these precious means of grace, the Holy Spirit keeps our faith in Jesus strong so we will be ready whenever God gives us the ultimate transfer—from earth to heaven!

Dear Father in Heaven

By calling Abraham to pull up stakes and head for the land of Your promise, You established your covenant with us. Thanks to Your loving grace, we are redeemed by Christ and washed clean. Deepen my trust in You and enable me to lead my family closer to You. In Jesus' name. Amen.

Today's Challenge

Remember God's promise to be with Abraham and share this promise with those who are moving away or who have recently moved into your area.

Saved by Faith Alone

Anyone not able to have children can relate to the emotions experienced by Abraham and his wife Sarah. Abraham had given up hope of having his own child. His wife Sarah was barren, and both of them were very old. Yet God promised Abraham many descendants. Although Abraham had given up on ever having children, he trusted God. And because of God's faithfulness, Abraham became the father of Isaac and a "spiritual nation" in which we are citizens. Moses wrote:

> And Abram said, "You have given me no children; so a servant in my household will be my heir." Then the word of the LORD came to him: "This man will not be your heir, but a son coming from your own body will be your heir. ... Look up at the heavens and count the stars—if indeed you can count them. ... So shall your offspring be." Abram believed the LORD, and He credited it to him as righteousness.
>
> *Genesis 15:3–6*

Years passed after God first called Abraham to move to the land He was going to give to Abraham's descendants. And still there were no descendants! Abraham remembered God's promise, but it was hard to rationally believe that he and his wife's aged bodies could give birth to a child. In these verses, we read that Abraham was prepared to pass his possessions on to a servant.

Then God revealed the most wonderful news Abraham could have heard, "'Look up at the heavens and count the stars—if indeed you can count them.' Then He said to him, 'So shall your offspring be.'" Instead of laughing or doubting the seemingly absurd promise, "Abram believed the Lord, and [the Lord] credited it to him as righteousness."

God had given a threefold promise to Abraham: 1. He would make him into a great nation, 2. His offspring will inherit the land, 3. All peoples on earth would be blessed through him. God, in His faithfulness, fulfilled all three.

God fulfilled the second part of His promise by leading Moses and the Israelites out of Egypt and into the Promised Land. Once the first two parts of God's promise were in place, God could joyfully take care of part three—sending His Son Jesus Christ for our salvation. Jesus alone kept the Law of God perfectly during His life on earth. He then went to the cross as the Lamb of God to be the one perfect offering for the sin of the whole world. In faith we join with Abraham in receiving our eternal inheritance.

As fathers, God calls us to a great responsibility—leading our family into the arms of Jesus. He enables us to fulfill this responsibility as we take our family to church every week and live a life of faith in Christ alone!

Lord Jesus

I am saved by faith alone in You. Grant me an ever increasing measure of Your Spirit along with a hunger to hear more of Your Word and to receive Your life-giving Supper. In Your name. Amen.

Today's Challenge

If you have been blessed with children, thank God for these marvelous gifts in your life!

Read Psalm 15
Deuteronomy 5

Absolutely

"Absolutely!" When we give this one word answer, we intend that what we are saying or agreeing with is the absolute truth. We want to be taken seriously, and we don't like it when we're not. Yet, in postmodern times, a lack of moral absolutes has emerged. To many, the distinction between right and wrong has been blurred.

In today's lesson from Deuteronomy, God calls sinners to trust in the absolute value He places on His Ten Commandments as the final word on what is right and wrong. Moses records:

> Moses summoned Israel and said: Hear, O Israel, the decrees and laws I declare in your hearing today. Learn them and be sure to follow them. ... These are the commandments the Lord proclaimed in a loud voice to your whole assembly there on the mountain from out of the fire, the cloud and the deep darkness; and He added nothing more.
>
> *Deuteronomy 5:1, 22*

Assuming you know the Ten Commandments are more than an old movie starring Charlton Heston, permit me to begin with the concluding remarks of Moses at the end of today's lesson, "These are the commandments the Lord proclaimed in a loud voice ... and He added nothing more." In a desire to apply the Ten Commandments, more than 600 additional laws were added. When Jesus came to earth to live among us, He condemned man's sinful practice of misusing God's Law to justify ourselves. "'These people honor me with their lips, but their hearts are far from Me. They worship Me in vain; their teachings are but rules taught by men'" (Matthew 15:8–9).

God gave 10 perfect commandments to govern our attitude and conduct toward God and other people. These Commandments are summarized by Jesus in this way, "'Love the Lord your God with all your heart and with all your soul and with all your mind.' This is the first and greatest commandment. And the second is like it: 'Love your neighbor as yourself.' All the Law and the Prophets hang on these two commandments" (Matthew 22:37–40).

Indeed, it is impossible for us to keep all of the commandments. James said, "For whoever keeps the whole law and yet stumbles at just one point is guilty of breaking all of it" (James 2:10). Although 10 in number, the commandments are *one* perfect Law of God, and we stand accused of absolute sinfulness.

Society's lack of moral absolutes reflects the sinful desire that seeks to divide and conquer God's Law by redefining what is good and what is evil according to human standards, not God's. As long as people can convince themselves that they are basically good by their own standards, they feel justified in that self-deception. Fortunately, it was for sin that Christ came to be our Savior.

Jesus Christ freed us from this sinful behavior by fulfilling the law. Because He died on the cross in our place, we no longer stand accused. He was absolutely perfect, so our salvation by grace through faith in Him is absolutely certain. His resurrection from the dead guarantees this promise. By the power of the Holy Spirit through our Baptism, the Word, and the Lord's Supper our hearts are inspired to please God through obedience.

Strengthened by faith, dads can commit to instructing their children that God means what He says in His Law—and in His Gospel. In Christ we are freed from the slavery of sin. Through faith we live out this freedom in willing obedience, knowing that all of our sins are forgiven through Christ's absolute love!

Heavenly Father

Through Your holy Law in the Ten Commandments, You revealed to me what is absolutely right and what is wrong. Forgive me for the times I have broken these commandments, and wash away all my sins for Your Son, Jesus', sake. In Jesus' precious name. Amen.

Today's Challenge

Review the Ten Commandments with your wife and children. As a family, discuss what each commandment means (Luther's Small Catechism is an excellent resource.)

Dad Means Teacher

My primary goal for writing this book is summarized in today's lesson. As a pastor, I have observed many men who have not taken their responsibility as the spiritual head of their family seriously. Yet although many husbands and fathers do not think their role includes leading their wives and children to worship, God holds men accountable for the spiritual welfare of their families. While this news is indeed serious, there's no need to panic. God wants you to enjoy your role as you watch the Lord draw your family closer to Him for all eternity. Within this context, the name "dad" leads to "teacher." Moses wrote:

> Love the LORD your God with all your heart and with all your soul and with all your strength. These commandments that I give you today are to be upon your hearts. Impress them on your children. Talk about them when you sit at home and when you walk along the road, when you lie down and when you get up. Tie them as symbols on your hands and bind them on your foreheads. Write them on the doorframes of your houses and on your gates.
>
> *Deuteronomy 6:5–9*

Today, the attitude toward being the family's spiritual leader can be compared to the attitude toward work in general. In the beginning, God put Adam and Eve in the Garden of Eden to work the land of His garden paradise. Work was part of God's creation, and it was good, like everything else God made. When sin came into the picture, however, the joy of work was turned into hard toil and labor. Because of sin, taking on the role of spiritual head of the household might be viewed as work. At times, taking our wives and children to worship and leading family devotions can appear to be one of the least exciting things to do with our families.

Despite this attitude, God still loves us. He has chosen us, our wives, and our children to be His own. He has placed us into His family with other believers in Christ, past and present. God wants to bestow unspeakable joy upon us on the Last Day when we are gathered before Him along with generations of our loved ones in Christ.

That's where today's lesson comes in, "These commandments that I give you today are to be upon your hearts. Impress them on your children. Talk about them when you sit at home and when you walk along the road, when you lie down and when you get up."

Our need to hear the Good News of God's grace through Jesus is greater than we can imagine. Just like us, our children face an eternity in one of two places—heaven or hell. God wants both our children and us to spend eternity with Him in heaven. Because God loves us, our rooms in heaven have already been paid for with the precious blood of God's Son who suffered and died on the cross.

That's where you come in as head of the household. Are your children baptized? Are you and your wife baptized? Are you taking your wife and children to worship every week? Are you going to the Lord's Supper as often as it is offered? Do you sprinkle your speech with the Gospel of Jesus? Is your faith in Jesus reflected in your daily actions? Difficult? Yes! Rewarding? Absolutely! Trust that God will strengthen and empower you to keep on learning so you can keep on teaching.

Heavenly Father

At times I have fallen short of my responsibility of teaching Your Word to my children. Please forgive me for Jesus' sake. Give me strength by Your Spirit to tell my family what Jesus has done for us and direct our paths in service to You. In Jesus' name. Amen.

Today's Challenge

Renew your commitment to your family by setting aside time for home devotions. Have fun talking about our wonderful God in Jesus' name.

Read Psalm 81
Deuteronomy 8:1–5

Disciplined Disciples

The word *discipline* evokes various images in my mind. I see a boy sitting in a "time out" chair, kids lined up in desks for school detention, a highway patrolman writing a traffic ticket, or even men behind bars in prison. Maybe you see highly polished U.S. Marines in their dress blues, white gloves, and glistening swords, or the split-second precision aerobatics of the U.S. Navy's Blue Angels fighter squadron.

Today's devotion delivers a message about life that might really surprise you. Keep in mind that the root word for *discipline* is *disciple*. Moses wrote:

> Remember how the LORD your God led you all the way in the desert these forty years, to humble you and to test you in order to know what was in your heart, whether or not you would keep His commands. He humbled you, causing you to hunger and then feeding you with manna, which neither you nor your fathers had known, to teach you that man does not live on bread alone but on every word that comes from the mouth of the LORD. Your clothes did not wear out and your feet did not swell during these forty years. Know then in your heart that as a man disciplines his son, so the LORD your God disciplines you.
>
> *Deuteronomy 8:2–5*

The book of Deuteronomy is the farewell sermon of Moses to the Israelites. In this sermon, Moses recounts all of the mighty works God performed for Israel after their deliverance from slavery in Egypt. As Moses prepared them for what would follow, he urged them to remember the testimonies of God's love.

As Moses recounted the hardships Israel endured while wandering in the wilderness, God was pointing out that He had used the hardships to draw them closer to Him, "Know then in your heart that as a man disciplines his son, so the LORD your God disciplines you."

What were the benefits of suffering? God says, "[I] humbled you, causing you to hunger and then feeding you with manna ... to teach you that man does not live on bread alone but on every word that comes from the mouth of the LORD."

As a loving Father, He also disciplines us as disciples. The author of the letter to the Hebrews put it this way, "Endure hardship as discipline; God is treating you as sons ... that we may share in His holiness. No discipline seems pleasant at the time, but painful. Later on, however, it produces a harvest of righteousness and peace for those who have been trained by it" (Hebrews 12:7–11).

God's promise encourages us not to become angry with Him in times of pain and suffering, but instead to ask for strength to bear our afflictions, trusting in His perfect love for us.

Moses also refers to humility. Although hard to admit, suffering benefits our souls. A life without pain and suffering would result in a shallow and self-serving life that could only lead to the curse of trusting in ourselves. We would likely tell God, "Lord, I thought I needed you, but I was wrong. I like being in charge, so I'll check back in if I need you." But God's discipline humbles us and helps us grow in dependence on Him.

Because of sin, suffering is never easy. Consider that Jesus, God's only Son, was put under discipline on this earth just as we are. Hebrews said, "Although He was a Son, He learned obedience from what He suffered and, once made perfect, He became the source of eternal salvation for all who obey Him" (Hebrews 5:8–9).

In Baptism, God mysteriously unites us with Christ in His death and resurrection, inviting us to trust in the discipline of the Holy Spirit to always lead us to the cross and open tomb as the source of our comfort and encouragement in times of suffering and hardship. As we gather with our family around God's Word and His Supper, Christ builds up our strength to trust in Him instead of in ourselves, so we can walk humbly, both before both God and with our fellow disciples.

Heavenly Father

I am Your son because Jesus is my Savior. Keep me mindful that through my suffering I am humbled before You. Forgive my sin and draw me ever closer to You. In Jesus' name. Amen.

Today's Challenge

When burdens and hardships come, ask God for strength to bear them. Talk to your pastor and seek to learn what lessons God might be teaching you.

WHO'S IT GOING TO BE?

Have you ever given your child the opportunity to choose a piece of candy from one of those really long candy displays? If you have, then you know that a "kid in a candy store" can be quite an investment of time. Many men have an equally difficult time deciding on one item as they stand in front of a display of fishing lures. Compare these two illustrations to the investment of time many women put into their shopping decisions.

These times of deliberation can be frustrating, but they are basically harmless. However, there is one kind of indecision that is eternally harmful. Turning to Joshua, the successor to Moses, we find God pressing the Israelites for a decision to the question, "Who's it going to be?" Joshua wrote:

> Now fear the LORD and serve Him with all faithfulness. Throw away the gods your forefathers worshiped beyond the River and in Egypt, and serve the LORD. But if serving the LORD seems undesirable to you, then choose for yourselves this day whom you will serve, whether the gods your forefathers served beyond the River, or the gods of the Amorites, in whose land you are living. But as for me and my household, we will serve the LORD.
>
> *Joshua 24:14–15*

Most of us are frustrated by politicians who never take a stand on issues—changing their spiel to match what their audience wants to hear. When people try to please everyone, they end up pleasing no one. The same principle applies in our relationship with God. Even after Israel entered the Promised Land, they continued to show only a halfhearted commitment to the Lord. All along, unless God was offering a visible performance at that moment (parting the Red Sea, making Mt. Sinai shake and smoke, bringing down the walls of Jericho, etc.), the Israelites were wishy-washy in their faith. At times they were downright hostile to God, preferring the false gods of other nations over the one true God.

In his own farewell address, Joshua echoed the same message as Moses—stay faithful to the Lord. Joshua urges those sitting on the fence of indecision to get off the fence and take a stand—either *for* the Lord or *against* Him.

Thankfully, there was no indecision in God's heart when He committed Himself to saving us! Although our Lord Jesus knew what the crown of thorns, the Roman scourge, and the cross would do to His own body, Jesus would not turn away from the mission He had come to earth to complete. He lived the perfect life in our place, then offered Himself up for the guilt and the punishment of the whole world's sin.

The Holy Spirit delivered this commitment of God to us in our Baptism, creating the gift of saving faith in our hearts. Jesus said, "You did not choose Me, but I chose you" (John 15:16). Only through the Spirit's power working through the Word and the sacraments are we able to make choices *for* God instead of *against* Him.

Whether it be in a the candy store, a favorite sport shop, or a women's clothing department, indecision is frustrating. When it comes to making a stand for the Lord, God's decision to love and forgive us for the sake of Christ leads us to rejoice. We realize anew that we can join with

Joshua saying, "As for me and my household, we will serve the Lord!"

Heavenly Father

Since You have chosen me through the gift of Your grace, fill me with desire to serve only You. When faced with tempting choices to turn away from You, strengthen me by the power of Your Holy Spirit to always choose what pleases You. In Jesus' name. Amen.

Today's Challenge

Are there material things or earthly goals getting between you and the Lord? Reinstate God and His Word as the top priority for you and your family. You will be eternally grateful.

Always Fathers

Most of the things we consume have an expiration date: meat, dairy products, and medicines. Even gasoline gets stale after a while. There are some things in this life, however, that never expire: our marriage, the relationship with our parents, and the relationship with our children. Although the roles we play in this life change with the passing years, the relationship of father to child remains, especially the relationship of the perfect Father to us, His children.

In today's devotion, we read about a unique man whose faithfulness to God continued to shine through His relationship with His children well after they grew up. From Job, we learn that we are always fathers. It is written:

> [Job] had seven sons and three daughters, and he owned seven thousand sheep, three thousand camels, five hundred yoke of oxen and five hundred donkeys, and had a large number of servants. He was the greatest man among all the people of the East. His sons used to take turns holding feasts in their homes, and they would invite their three sisters to eat and drink with them. When a period of feasting had run its course, Job would send and have them purified. Early in the morning he would sacrifice a burnt offering for each of them, thinking, "Perhaps my children have sinned and cursed God in their hearts." This was Job's regular custom.
>
> *Job 1:2–5*

Job had quite a portfolio. He probably worked hard, and with the Lord's blessing enjoyed vast wealth. Still, I'm sure if we had been able to ask Job, he would have counted his family as his greatest earthly treasure. Job showed that he was always a father by being concerned about the spiritual welfare of his children: "When a period of feasting had run its course, Job would send and have them purified. Early in the morning he would sacrifice a burnt offering for each of them, thinking, 'Perhaps my children have sinned and cursed God in their hearts.' This was Job's regular custom" (Job 1:5).

Just as Job had grown-up kids, so too do our children remain our children long after they turn 18. My mom and dad still pray for me and my family every day. The older I get, the more I appreciate and enjoy the blessings that flow from those prayers. Even if age reverses the role of primary caregiver between parent and child, the relationship still remains that of parent to child.

We demonstrate the qualities of a faithful father like Job through concern for our children. When tempted to worry, we can put our energy into praying for them—their health, safety, general welfare, humility, etc. We can be available for them, showing an interest in what's important in their lives. And we should never be afraid to discipline. Children might not admit it, but they want to know the difference between acceptable and unacceptable behavior. Children need the structure and stability that rules and discipline provide. Most important, fathers should "train [their children] in the way [they] should go, and when [the children] grow old, [they] will not turn from it" (Proverbs 22:6).

The fuel for this kind of training comes only from God. The first step to putting our child on the path leading to eternal life is to give them, by the Holy Spirit, the gift of saving faith in Jesus as Savior through Holy Baptism. Once that saving faith is in their hearts, our job as fathers isn't done. They are like thirsty sponges, ready to soak up every precious Word of God that flows in worship, Sunday school, vacation Bible school, Christian day school, confirmation instruction, or midweek programs at church.

Job could only offer burnt offerings on behalf of his children for the forgiveness of their sins. We can lead our children to trust in the sacrificial offering of God Himself. Through faith in Jesus and His death on the cross for us, God's children of all ages will rise to eternal life as our Lord did on that first Easter morning. Showing our children that Jesus is important to us assures them that we are always their father on earth, but God is their Father in heaven.

Heavenly Father

Of all the duties I have as father, remind me that the most important is to lead my children to know Jesus. Help me to show the same loving concern for their eternal welfare as Your servant Job did for his children. In Jesus' name. Amen.

Today's Challenge

Let your children know that you pray for them every day.

A Song of Praise

Have you ever received praise for something you accomplished? Being lauded as praiseworthy is indeed a wonderful and exhilarating feeling. Praise, like love, is *bestowed* upon someone who receives it, and I don't think anyone minds when it's their turn. Yet praise for what we accomplish is fleeting. Today's lesson looks at two grateful people who bestowed their praise on the Lord.

After Zechariah and Elizabeth received the wonderful gift of a healthy baby boy, they lifted their praises to the Lord. When the Lord opened Zechariah's mouth, the Holy Spirit filled Zechariah with a song of great praise. Luke records:

> He has raised up a horn of salvation for us in the house of His servant David ... salvation from our enemies and from the hand of all who hate us—to show mercy to our fathers and to remember His holy covenant, the oath He swore to our father Abraham: to rescue us from the hand of our enemies, and to enable us to serve Him without fear in holiness and righteousness before Him all our days.
>
> *Luke 1:69–75*

Zechariah's song of praise was both reflective and prophetic. It gave all glory to God for showing mercy to Zechariah's forefathers and for keeping the Lord's holy covenant with Abraham. Zechariah thanked God for rescuing His people from their enemies, and for enabling His people to serve Him in holiness and righteousness.

Remember Abraham? We spent some time getting acquainted with him so we could come to appreciate and give glory to God for keeping His three-fold promise to Abraham. God gave a nation of descendants to Abraham and He led them into the Promised Land. Here we see Zechariah heralding with joy the Good News that God would fulfill the third part of His Old Testament promise to Abraham.

The angel of the Lord made a solemn oath to Abraham as he prepared to sacrifice His son Isaac. The angel of the Lord said, "'I swear by Myself, declares the LORD, that because you have done this and have not withheld your son, your only son, I will surely bless you and make your descendants as numerous as the stars in the sky and as the sand on the seashore. Your descendants will take possession of the cities of their enemies, and through your offspring all nations on earth will be blessed, because you have obeyed Me'" (Genesis 22:16–18).

The offspring of Abraham had indeed multiplied and taken possession of the cities of their enemies. Now the whole world would be blessed by the birth of the perfect Israelite, Jesus of Nazareth. Only the blood of the innocent, spotless Lamb of God could wash away the sins of all the nations on earth. Jesus was sacrificed on the altar of the cross. Praise be to God that Jesus has indeed rescued us from the hand of our enemies. Through the precious means of grace, the Holy Spirit now enables us to serve the Lord without fear, in holiness and righteousness before Him all our days.

Zechariah turned to his infant son and glorified God for John's special career, "And you, my child, will be called a prophet of the Most High; for you will go on before the

Lord to prepare the way for Him, to give His people the knowledge of salvation through the forgiveness of their sins, because of the tender mercy of our God, by which the rising sun will come to us from heaven to shine on those living in darkness and in the shadow of death, to guide our feet into the path of peace" (Luke 1:76-79).

We all have special places in the kingdom of God. By the power of the Holy Spirit, we are eager to "declare the praises of Him who called [us] out of darkness into His wonderful light" (1 Peter 2:9). You can declare this wonderful news to your wife and children, and then to all whom you know. The message of Christ crucified and risen is our continuing song of praise!

Praise Be to You Forever, Oh Lord

You sent Your Son Jesus to redeem me from all my sins, shining the Light of heaven upon my family so we might walk in the path of Your peace. Shine through me so my family may see You in my actions. In Jesus' name. Amen.

Today's Challenge

Think about your daily routine and activities. How do you and your family reflect the "Light from heaven" in your lives?

Real Men Know What Their Families Need

Earlier we explored what a "real man" is in the eyes of the world. Although God says that real men run away from those things that bring spiritual and eternal death, He also says there are those things to which God wants real men to run. God wants us to always run to Him. According to God, real men also take their families to God's forgiving arms in worship. Having recently read about the amazing events surrounding the birth of John the Baptist, we can appreciate the grown-up John God presents as a mighty prophet to Israel. The apostle Matthew wrote:

> In those days John the Baptist came, preaching in the Desert of Judea and saying, "Repent, for the kingdom of heaven is near." This is he who was spoken of through the prophet Isaiah: "A voice of one calling in the desert, 'Prepare the way for the Lord, make straight paths for Him.'"
>
> *Matthew 3:1–3*

John's message from God was "Repent, for the kingdom of heaven is near." The word *repent* has three components. First, it means we feel sorrow because we have sinned against God. Second, repentance means we confess our sin and admit our sorrow to God and to those against whom we have sinned. Finally, we believe with all our hearts that God has forgiven us our sins.

John was sent ahead by God to prepare the way for the Lord, and to make straight the paths set before Him as the prophet Isaiah foretold. These straight paths are the paths of the heart. John was sent to level the hills of arrogance and pride that prevent people from seeing their need for total dependence on God for a Savior. At the same time, John's work required filling in the valleys of people's despair with the comfort of God's forgiving love and the promise of salvation through the coming Redeemer. John prepared the way for that Redeemer, the Son of God, Jesus Christ our Lord.

The Good News John proclaimed was that the coming Savior was physically on His way to fulfill the promise God had made to Abraham. Once this life-giving message was delivered by the Holy Spirit through John, people believed and were baptized. Matthew wrote, "People went out to him from Jerusalem and all Judea and the whole region of the Jordan. Confessing their sins, they were baptized by him in the Jordan River." I can only hope that the husbands led their wives and children from the security of the city out into the desert so they too might repent and be baptized in the Jordan.

Nearly 2,000 years later, fathers and husbands carry out the same responsibility as they set the alarm clock on Sunday morning (regardless how late they were up the night before), and get their children up, dressed, and out the door in time for worship.

Some parents may not want to attend church because they fear their infants or very young children might disrupt the service. However, there's no need for these parents to avoid attending church. Many of us have been in the same situation ourselves, and I'm sure those who haven't had children are more than willing to exercise a little Christian love and patience. Also, the more consistently young children attend church, the more familiar they will become with the liturgy, the routines, and expected behaviors and the more they will participate in worship.

Participating in worship is important because that is where God promises to be. And even though God is with us wherever we go, He comes to us in a very special way through the divine service to inspire us with His love and mercy in Jesus Christ. Through His means of grace, God forgives our sins and strengthens our faith. God has promised men and women everywhere, "Never will I leave you; never will I forsake you" (Hebrews 13:5). God will always provide the faith you and your family need.

Lord Jesus

You sent John ahead of You to prepare Your way. Now that You have come and taken my sins to the cross, help me, by Your Spirit's power, to point my wife and children to You as the only way to everlasting life. In Your name. Amen.

Today's Challenge

Resolve to be a "real man" according to the Bible's definition. Pray for the Holy Spirit's strength and guidance as you take on this endeavor.

Read Psalm 76
Luke 2:1–7

What Ancient Joseph Can Teach Modern Man

Although most will marvel at the architectural wonders of the Egyptians and praise the philosophical thinking of the ancient Greeks, many today would argue that our present society is the most advanced of all time. Judging by our tremendous technological advances, this argument seems difficult to dispute. But is there something we can yet learn from our ancestors?

In today's lesson, we turn to Matthew chapter one. Joseph was a faithful Israelite. He believed God's Word and looked forward to the promised Messiah. Read what happened when Joseph learned that his fiancée was pregnant, though he had never been intimate with her:

> Because Joseph her husband was a righteous man and did not want to expose her to public disgrace, he had in mind to divorce her quietly. But after he had considered this, an angel of the Lord appeared to him in a dream and said, "Joseph son of David, do not be afraid to take Mary home as your wife, because what is conceived in her is from the Holy Spirit. She will give birth to a Son, and you are to give Him the name Jesus, because He will save His people from their sins." ... When Joseph woke up, he did what the angel of the Lord had commanded him and took Mary home as his wife. But he had no union with her until she gave birth to a Son. And he gave Him the name Jesus.
>
> *Matthew 1:19–25*

Jesus was conceived by the Holy Spirit. If Joseph had been the biological father, Jesus would not have been the Son of God. Instead, He would have been born into sin, unable to free us from its bondage. Although Joseph was not the biological father, he demonstrated the biblical "real man" status we've come to appreciate by trusting in God and obeying the Lord's command. In so doing, Joseph lovingly provided for Mary and Jesus.

As the spiritual head of our households, we are accountable to God. Yet, in sin, we often fail. The Good News is that Jesus died on the cross to forgive us for all the times we have failed to assume responsibility for the spiritual welfare of our family. By the power of the Holy Spirit working through His means of grace, we can faithfully assume this awesome responsibility, and depend on God for guidance just like Joseph. Through Christ we are given strength to learn from the example of Joseph and love as "real men" in the Lord.

Heavenly Father

By Your grace, You gave Joseph the honor of caring for the needs of our Lord Jesus Christ. Just as Joseph was faithful to his role to raise Your Son during His life on earth, help us to raise Your dear children to know and love You. In Jesus' name. Amen.

Today's Challenge

Look at each of your children. Pause to think about how each is really a son or daughter of your heavenly Father. With His Spirit's help, raise your children to know God.

Read Psalm 85
Luke 2:8–20

Who Needs Laptops and Flip-phones?

How many of you have a laptop computer? How many of you have a flip-phone or another style of cellular phone? A third of you are probably thinking, *Yeah, I've got both. Wouldn't be without either.* Another third are probably thinking, *I don't have either one. Who needs 'em?* Still, the remaining third are probably thinking, *I don't have either, but I would sure like to!*

It's an amazing era in which we live. Information can now be transferred from one place to another literally at the speed of light. I chuckle a little when I get frustrated for having to wait a whole minute to get something off the Internet, when a trip to the library for the same information would easily be a half-hour commitment!

When it comes to the transfer of God's saving grace that brings eternal life, thank God that the Holy Spirit's method of *data transfer* is very *user-friendly.* Turning to the Christmas story, we see that the shepherds got by exceedingly well without laptops and flip-phones. After the angels had told the shepherds of Jesus' birth, they immediately went to the manger. The account in Luke reads:

> When [the shepherds] had seen [Jesus], they spread the word concerning what had been told them about this Child, and all who heard it were amazed at what the shepherds said to them. ... The shepherds returned, glorifying and praising God for all the things they had heard and seen, which were just as they had been told.
>
> *Luke 2:17–20*

What would the Christmas story be without the shepherds? God handpicked these men to be the very first recipients of the news the faithful world had been waiting to hear since Adam and Eve first brought sin into the world.

Thank God we weren't in charge of writing the Christmas story. If we had been in charge, our Savior probably would have been like any other king on earth—self-seeking, glory-grabbing, and sinful. But Jesus was unlike any earthly king. He was true God and true man. His humble birth in a stable and the announcement made to lowly shepherds set the tone for the remainder of His blessed, perfect life of humility before God and humankind.

The shepherds received the message of Jesus' birth with joy. As they did not have e-mail or cell phones, they used their feet and mouths to declare the Good News to everyone around them. God has sent His Son into the world as Savior! God can use us too as His messengers on earth.

We don't need laptops or cell phones to transmit the Good News of salvation through Christ. The angels' announcement to the shepherds is made ours through the precious means of grace: Baptism, God's Word, and the Lord's Supper. With the same joy of the shepherds, may you and your family use your mouths and feet to tell the world of Christ's undying love.

Heavenly Father

You have given me the eyes of faith with which to see Jesus as my Savior and a voice to proclaim Him to others. Work through me to tell others around me about You—the God who became man to save the world from its sins. In Jesus' name. Amen.

Today's Challenge

May you and your family keep the story of Christmas alive throughout the whole year, not just in December.

Always on Call, Ready for Duty!

Do you like waking up in the middle of the night to go somewhere? (Probably only when you are leaving for a fishing or hunting trip.) As a firefighter, I can assure you that hearing the siren and the pager go off at 2:00 A.M. in January when it's zero degrees outside is not my favorite thing. In fact, 2:00 A.M. at any time of the year is never a pleasant time to wake up and be on your way! However, firefighters are always on call and ready for duty.

You don't have to be a firefighter to know the weariness of climbing out of bed when you'd rather stay there. Joseph, the stepfather of Jesus, knew what it was like to get up in the middle of the night. While he didn't get up to save someone's house from a fire, Joseph got up to save the life of Jesus, the Son of God. As dads consider this event from our Lord's early life, they need to remember this important lesson: Satan has his eyes set on your family, and if you don't look to help from the Lord for their spiritual needs, who will? Matthew wrote:

> When [the Wise Men] had gone, an angel of the Lord appeared to Joseph in a dream. "Get up," he said, "take the child and his mother and escape to Egypt. Stay there until I tell you, for Herod is going to search for the child to kill Him." So he got up, took the child and His mother during the night and left for Egypt, where He stayed until the death of Herod.
>
> *Matthew 2:13–15*

To appreciate what Joseph was up against, it helps to know something about King Herod. "Herod the Great" ruled over Judea and Galilee from 37–4 B.C. He was an extremely jealous king and eliminated anyone who posed the slightest threat to his throne—even members of his own family!

When the Wise Men came to ask Herod about the new King of the Jews, Herod immediately began plotting Jesus' demise. He asked the Wise Men to report to him when they found Jesus, saying that he wanted to worship the newborn King. But God warned the Wise Men in a dream of Herod's plan to kill Jesus, so they were careful to avoid the evil king on the way back to their own country.

Because Herod could not know which baby boy was the newborn King, he killed all the baby boys two years old and younger to eliminate the perceived threat to his power. The mass murder of these baby boys is commemorated on December 28 as "The Holy Innocents, Martyrs."

Although our Lord was spared death at that time in His life due to God's warning, His life would not be spared forever. He fulfilled the Law on our behalf, and he voluntarily went to the chief priests and teachers of the Law, who condemned Him for blasphemy against God's Word. Then Jesus was mocked and sentenced by Pontius Pilate for crucifixion.

Since our Lord suffered and died to pay for a world of sins and has risen victorious, we trust that one day we too will rise and live forever as grateful subjects and children of our Savior and King! Until that Day, men must keep a watchful eye for temptations and other dangers Satan sets before their families.

What is your protection against these spiritual hazards? Fear not, for the Holy Spirit has created saving faith in your heart through Baptism. God also arms you with

His Word and the precious sin-forgiving, faith-strengthening food of Christ's true body and blood in the Lord's Supper. Through these means of grace, the Holy Spirit equips husbands and fathers to nurture the spiritual lives of their families. Always on call, ready for duty!

Heavenly Father

Thank You for sending Your Son as my Savior from sin. Arm me against Satan's attacks and enable me to lead my family into the saving grace at Your loving arms. In Jesus' name. Amen.

Today's Challenge

The next time you have to get up in the middle of the night, think of Joseph. Ask the Lord to bless you with the willingness and trust He bestowed upon Joseph.

Read Psalm 119:1–8
Luke 2:41–52

God's Word—Who Needs It?

Who in your life needs to hear God's Word the least. Would it be your mother? Your dad? Your pastor? Could it be your wife? Could it be you? Obviously, your kids need to hear God's Word. Is there anyone who *does not* need to hear God's Word as much as others? How about Jesus? He certainly doesn't need to hear God's Word because He *is* God's Word. Yet, even Jesus showed the need to hear God's Word during His life on earth.

As we turn to today's lesson from Luke chapter two, we find out just how much Jesus knew about God's Word— even as a 12-year-old boy. St. Luke wrote:

> After the Feast was over, while His parents were returning home, the boy Jesus stayed behind in Jerusalem, but they were unaware of it. Thinking He was in their company, they traveled on for a day. Then they began looking for Him among their relatives and friends. When they did not find Him, they went back to Jerusalem to look for Him. After three days they found Him in the temple courts, sitting among the teachers, listening to them and asking them questions. Everyone who heard Him was amazed at His understanding and His answers.
>
> *Luke 2:43–47*

This is the only recorded portion of our Lord's life between His return from Egypt as a toddler and His Baptism as an adult in the Jordan River. St. Luke's inclusion of this event illustrates our Lord's priorities as a 12-year-old boy. Most 12-year-old boys today are focused on sports or hobbies. But Jesus was focused on something else.

Jesus came with His family in their annual pilgrimage to Jerusalem to celebrate the Passover. When the Passover was over, they packed up and headed home with their caravan of friends and family. The fact that Mary and Joseph did not see Jesus until that evening is of no more surprise when we consider what it would be like if our children were with their cousins and friends playing at a large family get-together. Mary and Joseph started casually asking, "Have you seen Jesus?" Panic must have set in when it became clear that He was not in their company.

Three days later Mary and Joseph found Jesus in the temple courts, sitting among the teachers. Everyone who heard Jesus was amazed. Even as a young boy, our Lord was completely focused on His Heavenly Father's plan for Him. When Mary and Joseph found Jesus, He asked them, "Didn't you know I had to be in My Father's house?" (Luke 2:49).

Our Lord made a return trip to Jerusalem during Passover 21 years later. This time He entered with much attention, causing quite a stir throughout the city. People shouted, "Hosanna! Blessed is He who comes in the name of the Lord!" However, the end of the week their shouts changed to "Crucify Him! Crucify Him!" The teachers at whose feet Jesus had sat and listened, and who had been amazed at the promise of this young man, would have their own colleagues decry Jesus saying, "He saved others, ... but He can't save Himself!" (Matthew 27:42).

Our Lord hungered throughout His entire life for God's Word. He preached in the synagogue and frequently withdrew to quiet places to talk to His heavenly Father in prayer. Prior to His death on the cross, Christ instituted the Lord's Supper so we might be united with Him through His death. Following His resurrection, Jesus instituted the office of the holy ministry with the responsibility for feeding so His lambs might be fed on God's Word. Christ gave all of this to His Church on earth for the forgiveness of our sins until the day He returns to raise us from the dead and take us to be with Him forever in heaven!

We all need the saving message of God's Word! Share the Word with everyone you know, especially the members of your family.

Heavenly Father

Fill me with a hunger for Your Word and a thirst for the righteousness that is mine through the blood of Your Son shed for me. In His precious name. Amen.

Today's Challenge

Read this account from Luke's gospel to your children. Ask them what Jesus meant when He said "Why were you searching for me? Didn't you know I had to be in my Father's house?" Talk about your opportunities to come to the house of the Lord.

The Ultimate Waste of Time

Do you like to waste time? Probably not. Not many of us do. The more compelling question is, *"Do you waste time?"* Probably so. Mastering the skill of time management is a lifelong pursuit. Very few people are self-disciplined enough to achieve such a goal. What are the things in your life that prevent you from making good use of your time? Have you lost your calendar or date book? Are you unorganized? Are you easily distracted?

The Bible tells us that worrying is the chief way people waste their time. Perhaps you never thought of worrying as a waste of time, but it is. God does not want us to worry. In today's lesson from the gospel of Matthew, our Lord Jesus tells us not to worry is because we're in good hands. Matthew wrote:

> So do not worry, saying, "What shall we eat?" or "What shall we drink?" or "What shall we wear?" For the pagans run after all these things, and your heavenly Father knows that you need them. But seek first His kingdom and His righteousness, and all these things will be given to you as well. Therefore do not worry about tomorrow, for tomorrow will worry about itself. Each day has enough trouble of its own.
>
> *Matthew 6:31–34*

The advice to not worry is common. Giving a good reason for why you shouldn't worry is not so common. Our Lord has a joyously real reason for not worrying that goes beyond the ups and downs of living in this sinful world. God, in His divine and perfect wisdom, is in control of the seemingly chaotic world in which we live. Once you believe in the salvation Jesus earned for you on the cross, nothing in this world should cause you to worry. You are a saved child of God with the promise of forgiveness and eternal life in heaven.

God identifies worry as a symptom of weak faith. He said, "If that is how God clothes the grass of the field, which is here today and tomorrow is thrown into the fire, will He not much more clothe you, O you of little faith?" (Matthew 6:30).

Thankfully, God gives us His means of grace to strengthen our faith when we begin to worry. Coming to worship helps strengthen our faith through the Holy Spirit's work in the hearts of the community of believers. Gradually our trust grows and our worry fades.

Our heavenly Father knows our needs far better than we do. After all, He sent Christ to the cross out of His eternal love for us. He always wants what's best for us. He gives us what we need even if we forget to ask Him or do not know what's best for us. Even if our worst fears are realized in this life, we can trust that God has provided a heavenly home for us free of all our worldly problems.

In the meantime, through His Word and sacraments, you can seek first God's kingdom and His righteousness, and God will shower many blessings upon you and your family (Matthew 6:33). Go out and share the Lord's time management secret with everyone you know!

Lord Jesus

Thank You for telling me why I need not worry. When I am tempted to worry, remind me that my heavenly Father knows all my needs and provides for me for Your name's sake. By Your Holy Spirit, fill me with the desire and strength to seek first Your kingdom and Your righteousness. In Your holy name. Amen.

Today's Challenge

Write out Matthew 6:25–34 on your computer or by hand and make several copies. Place the Bible passage in areas where you are tempted to worry (desk, checkbook, etc.) As you read the Bible passage, ask God for His help and reassurance. Then continue your day in peace as you stop wasting time in Jesus' name!

Read Psalm 149
Matthew 21:1–17

Out of the Mouths of Children

How many of you have been in situations where your kids opened their mouths and said something that totally embarrassed you? If you are not yet a parent, be careful who you laugh at! If you do become a parent, I can almost guarantee embarrassing things will happen to you! It's basically a law of parenthood.

The words that come out of a kid's mouth are frightening because they are the honest, unfiltered truth. Today, we're going to read about Jesus' triumphant entry into Jerusalem, and the honest praise Jesus heard that day from the mouths of children. Matthew wrote:

> The crowds that went ahead of [Jesus] and those that followed shouted, "Hosanna to the Son of David!" "Blessed is He who comes in the name of the Lord!" "Hosanna in the highest!" When Jesus entered Jerusalem, the whole city was stirred and asked, "Who is this?" The crowds answered, "This is Jesus, the prophet from Nazareth in Galilee." ... But when the chief priests and the teachers of the law saw the wonderful things He did and the children shouting in the temple area, "Hosanna to the Son of David," they were indignant. "Do you hear what these children are saying?" they asked Him. "Yes," replied Jesus, "have you never read, 'From the lips of children and infants You have ordained praise'?"
>
> *Matthew 21:9–16*

How did these people know what to do? How did they know that Jesus was the Son of David? Evidently, the people in the crowd knew the prophecies that identified the Savior as the Son of David who would ride into Jerusalem on a donkey. The prophet Zechariah foretold, "Rejoice greatly, O Daughter of Zion! Shout, Daughter of Jerusalem! See, your King comes to you, righteous and having salvation, gentle and riding on a donkey, on a colt, the foal of a donkey. I will take away the chariots from Ephraim and the war-horses from Jerusalem" (Zechariah 9:9–10a).

As the kingdom of the first son of David (Solomon) was marked by peace among men, so the eternal kingdom of Jesus (the true Messianic Son of David) would be established in peace between God and humans. The righteous King Jesus rode into Israel on a donkey instead of a war horse. The eternal kingdom of peace was established with a crown of thorns and a gauntlet of jeering crowds instead of a royal coronation. God's Anointed One carried His own cross to the place where He was finally nailed to it. On that cross, Jesus suffered the punishment for the sins of the whole world. Although Jesus knew from the beginning that all these terrible things lay ahead, He still accepted the praises of the crowd, especially the praises of the children.

The children were praising Jesus as the Son of David along with the adults. They joyfully shouted, "Hosanna," meaning "Lord save." As they praised Jesus as their Savior, the children fulfilled the ancient prophecies that credited the children's praise as the sweetest and purest Jesus could receive. Jesus praised the children because of their humble faith. He said, "I tell you the truth, unless you change and become like little children, you will never enter the kingdom of heaven. Therefore, whoever humbles himself like this child is the greatest in the kingdom of heaven" (Matthew 18:3–4).

Looking at our own children today who so sweetly confess the name of Jesus, may we learn to follow their example of pure, humble praise. Nurtured by our Baptism into Christ's death and resurrection, may we also grow in faith with our children. By the power of His Holy Spirit, let us build a faithful life around Christ's Word and worship all the days of our lives. Someday, we too will wave our palms before Christ in the glory of heaven.

Hosanna in the Highest, Lord Jesus! Blessed is Your Name Forever and Ever!

Thank You for coming to my rescue with Your perfect life and innocent suffering and death in my place. Help me to always teach my wife and children of Your great love so we will be with You forever. In Your holy name. Amen.

Today's Challenge

If you have children, thank God for their simple trust and natural inclination to speak the truth. Fill them up with the truth of Jesus so they can honestly share the Good News with others.

Your Real Family

Do you *like* everyone in your family? Even the in-laws? Unless you are extraordinarily blessed, chances are there is someone in your family with whom you don't see eye to eye. Different personalities and diverse experiences particular to individuals almost guarantee there will be some relatives you like more than others.

However, even if you don't *like* everyone in your family (as in Webster's definition, to take pleasure in), you can *love* them (as in God's definition). God commands us to love everyone, including our enemies and strange family members. To both *like and love* is a blessing and joy shared between dear loved ones and friends. Yet in some homes, conflicts arise that prevent this joy.

For example, conflicts can occur when some family members believe in Jesus, some don't believe at all, and others are wavering and uncertain in their faith. Today we go to the official birthday of the Christian Church, Pentecost. Here we witness the beginning of the family of faith—conflicts and all. St. Luke wrote:

> Those who accepted [Peter's] message were baptized, and about three thousand were added to their number that day. They devoted themselves to the apostles' teaching and to the fellowship [public worship], to the breaking of bread and to prayer. Everyone was filled with awe, and many wonders and miraculous signs were done by the apostles. ... And the Lord added to their number daily those who were being saved.
>
> *Acts 2:41–47*

233

It was the day of Pentecost, an Old Testament festival celebrating the harvest. It was the fiftieth day since our Lord had risen from the dead, and ten days since He had bodily ascended into heaven. Jesus had left these instructions with His disciples: "Do not leave Jerusalem, but wait for the gift My Father promised, which you have heard Me speak about. For John baptized with water, but in a few days you will be baptized with the Holy Spirit" (Acts 1:4b–5).

Jews and converts to Judaism from all over the known world had gathered at Jerusalem to celebrate this festival. Little did these multitudes know the special plans God had that would give new meaning to this festival of the harvest!

After Jesus was arrested, condemned to die, and crucified for the sins of the whole world, the disciples of Jesus were terrified of what might happen to them. They stayed inside their meeting place and kept the doors locked. On the day of Pentecost, however, the disciples were given a wisdom and courage they had never known before.

With the new understanding and courage the Holy Spirit bestowed upon him, Peter gave a sermon to the crowds that yielded miraculous results. Those who heard the Word of God that day were especially blessed by the power of the Holy Spirit. Luke wrote, "Those who accepted [Peter's] message were baptized, and about three thousand were added to their number that day. They devoted themselves to the apostles' teaching and to the fellowship, to the breaking of bread and to prayer."

Rejoice if everyone in your family knows and loves the Lord Jesus! However, if some in your family do not yet know and love the Lord, pray for the Holy Spirit to give you courage and wisdom as you share the Good News with them. Pray that the Holy Spirit would open their hearts and bring them into God's gracious family.

God has provided an extended family for you in His church—your brothers and sisters in Christ. As you gather around God's Word and receive God's forgiveness, thank the Lord for the love and strength He gives you through His Christian family. May you, by the power of the Holy Spirit, help your wife and children experience the joyful unity of your family of faith *loving* even those you may not particularly *like*.

Oh Holy Spirit

As You gave faith and courage to the apostles on that first Pentecost, so also give me the words to proclaim Jesus as my only Savior from sin. In Jesus' name. Amen.

Today's Challenge

The early Church grew by sharing the Gospel between family and friends. Ask the Holy Spirit for guidance and courage and go to work telling others!

Midnight Divine Service

A beautiful German word is *Gottesdienst*. The word translates to *divine service*. It means that God is literally serving us when we gather in His holy house for worship. God Himself comes to us and speaks to us through His Word. He claims us as His own through the waters of Baptism, feeds and nourishes us through His body and blood. Freed and forgiven, we build one another up as we speak to each other in psalms, hymns, and spiritual songs.

In our exciting lesson from Acts, we see a dramatic display of "divine service" in a jail at midnight. St. Luke wrote:

> About midnight Paul and Silas were praying and singing hymns to God, and the other prisoners were listening to them. Suddenly there was such a violent earthquake that the foundations of the prison were shaken. At once all the prison doors flew open, and everybody's chains came loose. The jailer woke up, and when he saw the prison doors open, he drew his sword and was about to kill himself because he thought the prisoners had escaped. But Paul shouted, "Don't harm yourself! We are all here!"
>
> *Acts 16:25–28*

Paul, Silas, and the rest of their company had been faithfully spreading the Word of God, proclaiming it both far and wide. The other prisoners in the jail might have expected Paul and Silas to cry out at the injustice of their imprisonment, saying, "It's not fair, God! How could you let them imprison us?" But Paul and Silas remained faithful, "praying and singing hymns to God." What a response! Paul and Silas knew that God was with them in that prison cell. They held in their hearts and minds the hymns, prayers, and Scripture they had faithfully learned.

It is crucial that husbands and dads worship with their families every week—gathered around God's Holy Word and God's means of grace, namely Baptism and the Lord's Supper. Freed and forgiven, psalms, hymns, and spiritual songs become an active expression of your thanks and praise for all that God has done for you through Jesus.

The earthquake that shook open the prison doors and loosened the prisoners' chains was not nearly as important as what happened next, "[The jailer] then brought [Paul and Silas] out and asked, 'Sirs, what must I do to be saved?' They replied, 'Believe in the Lord Jesus, and you will be saved—you and your household'" (Acts 16:30–31).

The "divine service" continued at the jailer's home, "At that hour of the night the jailer took them and washed their wounds; then immediately he and his family were baptized. The jailer brought them into his house and set a meal before them; he was filled with joy because he had come to believe in God—he and his whole family" (Acts 16:33–34). Through Holy Baptism, young and old alike received the gift of saving faith and the assurance they were now officially members of God's family as His Spirit entered their hearts.

God's greatest act of divine service occurred when He sent His Son Jesus to earth to die for the sins of the world. Because of Jesus' perfect life, death, and resurrection, all who believe in Jesus are saved and will have eternal life. Knowing that God serves us brings true joy into our hearts, a joy that naturally flows by the Spirit's presence in us. Let us express our gratitude in a life pleasing to God by reflecting His love and wisdom in our actions. All thanks to God for His continuing *Gottesdienst*!

Heavenly Father

You took great pleasure in getting the Good News of salvation through Your Son Jesus to the world. Help me, by Your Spirit's power, to spread this same news of salvation to my family, friends, coworkers, and all others You place in my life. In Jesus' name. Amen.

Today's Challenge

While in prison, Paul and Silas sang hymns they had committed to memory. Hymns are one of the church's great treasures. Buy a hymnal if you don't already have one and read the hymns. Pick out some favorites and memorize them so you can sing when you are driving, gardening, and so forth.

Authority has Accountability

You've probably heard the phrase "power corrupts." The movie *Mister Smith Goes to Washington* portrays corruption in the lives of elected government officials. Because of such real-life incidents, many Americans have begun to deride and scorn the entire political process. Sinful humans sometimes occupy political positions; consequently sinful decisions can be made or sinful acts performed. But to whom are they accountable?

In today's lesson, we find that we do not have to be elected officials to hold power and authority. With any power we hold comes the sobering message from God's Word that "authority has accountability." St. Paul wrote:

> Children obey your parents in the Lord, for this is right.
> ... Fathers, do not exasperate your children; instead, bring them up in the training and instruction of the Lord. Slaves, obey your earthly masters with respect and fear, and with sincerity of heart, just as you would obey Christ. ... And masters, treat your slaves in the same way. Do not threaten them, since you know that He who is both their Master and yours is in heaven, and there is no favoritism with Him.
>
> *Ephesians 6:1–9*

In this portion of Paul's letter to the Christians at Ephesus, he addresses four specific groups of people, but the same message applies to them all. The first group is children. God told children to obey their parents in the Lord.

God expressed His heartfelt desire that children show their parents honor and love. Children can never fully repay their debt of love to their parents who gave them life and raised them. There is no expiration date for this expression of love, so as adults, we also love and honor our parents all their days, especially if God has given parents extra years with their adult children.

The next group is dads. God said, "Fathers, do not exasperate your children." This passage could very easily be misinterpreted, especially in today's permissive culture. It simply means that fathers should not turn their children away from the Lord by abusing their authority over their children. Children should see Jesus in their fathers' lives. Fathers are called to attend weekly worship around God's means of grace with their children and wives. This is what God meant when He said, "Instead, bring [your children] up in the training and instruction of the Lord."

Although we don't technically have slaves and masters in our culture today, the last two groups can be considered to be employees and employers. Employees ought to submit to the authority of their bosses, not merely for their own sake, but for the Lord's sake. They are to act as if the Lord were giving them instructions, provided those instructions don't require the employee to do something sinful.

Employers are to treat their employees as the Lord treats them. Employers ought not let the authority they wield go to their heads. Instead, they should set a godly example by showing justice, compassion, and forgiveness. In doing so, perhaps coworkers will seek to know more about the employer's Lord and Master.

We look at the authority God has given us with holy fear and trembling. We ask God's Holy Spirit to fill us with wisdom, so we may give an account of our labors on the

Last Day with great joy and humble gratitude to our God and Savior—to whom we are accountable!

Heavenly Father

You are my Master. Remind me every day of what a great privilege it is to hold the offices and roles You have given me, especially my roles as husband, father, and son. Remind me that I am accountable to You for how I manage my responsibilities—especially my responsibility to lead my wife and children to Your arms through a life faithful to worship and Your means of grace. In Jesus' name. Amen.

Today's Challenge

Write down all the offices and roles you hold, then think about whose lives are affected. As part of your daily prayers, ask God for strength to perform to His glory the duties of those roles faithfully and with a humble heart.

Reactive Armor

Over coffee one day, one of the elders of my church and I discussed battle armor, such as that on tanks and armored personnel carriers. He mentioned something I had never heard of before—reactive armor. He explained that this armor does exactly what the name implies—it reacts. It breaks down upon contact with an incoming round, thereby reducing the overall impact of the attacker's shot.

That's when I realized I had, in fact, already heard of reactive armor. It's found in today's lesson from Ephesians. As we battle against our enemies—the devil, the world, and our own flesh—St. Paul reminds us that God equips us with His reactive armor—faith in His Word! Paul wrote:

> Therefore put on the full armor of God, so that when the day of evil comes, you may be able to stand your ground, and after you have done everything, to stand. Stand firm then, with the belt of truth buckled around your waist, with the breastplate of righteousness in place, and with your feet fitted with the readiness that comes from the gospel of peace. In addition to all this, take up the shield of faith, with which you can extinguish all the flaming arrows of the evil one. Take the helmet of salvation and the sword of the Spirit, which is the Word of God. And pray in the Spirit on all occasions with all kinds of prayers and requests.
>
> *Ephesians 6:13–18*

All Christians are soldiers in the battle Paul spoke of. This probably comes as no surprise since Scripture often speaks of Christians as soldiers. However, you may be surprised to know that the war is already over! Our great enemy, the devil, has been defeated. He was beaten 2,000 years ago when our Lord Jesus died on the cross, satisfying God's just anger over our innumerable sins. Jesus' resurrection from the dead has sealed our victory over Satan, sin, and death. That means heaven is our home right now!

The difficult part for us is the trip home. The devil has a scorched earth policy and will not yield a single inch until every last Christian soldier is taken out. The devil's soldiers—demons, other sinful people, and even our own weak flesh—are constantly taking pot shots at us, encouraging us to abandon making our trip home. In fact, the enemy is trying hard to seduce us into joining their defeated cause. This is where God's reactive armor comes in.

St. Paul wrote, "Stand firm then, with the belt of truth buckled around your waist, with the breastplate of righteousness in place, and with your feet fitted with the readiness that comes from the gospel of peace. In addition to all this, take up the shield of faith, with which you can extinguish all the flaming arrows of the evil one. Take the helmet of salvation and the sword of the Spirit, which is the Word of God" (Ephesians 6:14–17).

The order from our real Commander in Chief is to "Stand firm!" We can do this when we are connected with our "supply lines" via worship in the community of believers. Here, fellow soldiers acknowledge sin and are forgiven. We are strengthened through God's word and fortified in faith. The armor of God is firmly placed upon us.

With armor in place, we walk in confidence, knowing that our teaching is the truth. We know that we are perfect in God's sight, covered in the righteousness of His only

Son through faith. Our feet can march through this world in great readiness because the Gospel assures us that we are at peace with God. Finally, knowing that salvation is God's free gift, we have the joy to pray for our family, our friends, and all who are in God's victorious army. Let us press on to our heavenly home, safely clothed in our reactive armor.

Lord Jesus

Thank You for giving me Your Holy Spirit in my Baptism. I am now fully equipped with the armor of Your Word and the means of Your grace so I may enter into battle, knowing that, by Your death on the cross, the victory over sin is already mine! In Your name. Amen.

Today's Challenge

Examine your armor. Are there any chinks or vulnerable places in it? If so, allow your armor to be reinforced through God's Word and feeding on the Lord's Supper. Pray that the Holy Spirit would strengthen your faith through His means of grace. Ask that God would guide you and all believers on your journey home to heaven.

Read Psalm 122
James 2:1–13

Don't Play Favorites

Have you ever caught yourself playing favorites? Perhaps you've given one child an extra snack because she's just so cute. Maybe you have spent more time with your son than with your other children because you're so proud of his athletic ability and want to help him excel even more. If you had siblings, I'm sure you know how terrible it feels to be left out by a parent—even by accident. The seemingly forgotten children feel lonely and abandoned.

Knowing the pain favoritism causes, we can understand why God caused St. James to be so hard on those who played favorites in God's Church. St. James wrote:

> If you really keep the royal law found in Scripture, "Love your neighbor as yourself," you are doing right. But if you show favoritism, you sin and are convicted by the law as lawbreakers. For whoever keeps the whole law and yet stumbles at just one point is guilty of breaking all of it. ... Speak and act as those who are going to be judged by the law that gives freedom, because judgment without mercy will be shown to anyone who has not been merciful. Mercy triumphs over judgment!
>
> *James 2:8–13*

Favoritism is a sin the devil uses to divide Christ's Church. James chapter two gives an example of two visitors coming to a church. One man is clearly well off financially, while the other is not. When the rich man enters, many reason, "This fellow may be able to give a substantial amount each year to our offerings. Let's make him feel welcome so he'll come back and perhaps join our church." But when the poor man comes in, many think, "Oooh. Do we really want a person like that joining our church? He makes me feel uncomfortable. I mean, he might scare off potential middle and upper class members."

May God have mercy on us if such a thought passes through our minds for a split second! St. James wrote, "Have you not discriminated among yourselves and become judges with evil thoughts?" (James 2:4).

Jesus was sharply criticized because He loved all people the same. While He was on earth, God chose those who were poor in the eyes of the world to be rich in faith and to inherit His kingdom. Since Christ loves all people equally and has paid for all people's sins by His perfect life, suffering, and death on the cross, the issue of discrimination is settled—Christians don't need to discriminate either when it comes to deciding who they will love. In Christ, we are called to be merciful and loving toward everyone.

All who have been baptized into Christ have had their sins washed away and are equally precious in God's sight. As we gather around the Lord's Supper in worship and receive the true body and blood of Christ for the forgiveness of sins, so we also publicly confess our trust that, in God's eyes, we are all equal—redeemed brothers and sisters in Christ! By loving one another as God loved us, we send a clear message to the world that we belong to the God who does not judge according to outward appearance.

Empowered by His love, the words we say to church visitors and all who need God's love and grace include: "Welcome friend! We're glad you've joined us!" "Here is a bulletin. These are the times of our Bible studies and weekly activities." "Would you please sign our guest book? Could one of our members stop by some time and give you a little more information about our church? Could our pastor pay you a visit?"

Let us always remember that the cross and open tomb proclaim us all as "favorites" in God's eyes. May we be led by the Holy Spirit to show God's love equally to all, in our own family and within the family of believers.

Heavenly Father

You do not show favoritism as You call children into Your kingdom for You love us all the same. Help me, by Your Spirit's power, to love others in that same way. In Jesus' name. Amen.

Today's Challenge

Think about the people you know. Are there any you find yourself looking down upon? Reach out to this person in Christian love. Pray that the Holy Spirit would lead you to love and serve everyone equally.

Read Psalm 100
1 Peter 1:3–12

Making God's Goals Our Goals

A colleague of mine has observed that the trends of the business world eventually trickle down into the ways the church accomplishes the "business" aspects of ministry. Some of these trends include mission statements and understanding the culture of the church. One practice for success shared by business and church is that of setting goals. Children of God trust God's goals to be their goals in business, church, and at home. St. Peter wrote:

> Praise be to the God and Father of our Lord Jesus Christ! In His great mercy He has given us new birth into a living hope through the resurrection of Jesus Christ from the dead, and into an inheritance that can never perish, spoil or fade—kept in heaven for you, who through faith are shielded by God's power until the coming of the salvation that is ready to be revealed in the last time. In this you greatly rejoice, though now for a little while you may have had to suffer grief in all kinds of trials.
>
> *1 Peter 1:3–6*

As we live our lives on this earth with the power of God's Holy Spirit, our goal is to carry the cross of discipleship. This objective encompasses all the sufferings that come into our lives as a result of being a child of God through faith alone in Jesus Christ. We can endure ridicule, both mild and severe. This is why Peter says, "In this you greatly rejoice, though now for a little while you may have had to suffer grief in all kinds of trials."

Why would Christians rejoice when they suffer? Because Christians have another goal that lasts forever—long after our short time on this earth is past. Christians know that their life and possessions on earth are temporary. Through faith they trust that the suffering and pain of this life are also temporary—but the gift of salvation is eternal. Christians can rejoice at all times, even during severe persecution, because they are confident in the glorious inheritance God has prepared for them in heaven and confident in all the spiritual blessings God bestows on them during their life on earth.

Through hardship, God draws us closer to Himself as our source of strength. By ourselves, it is impossible to live the perfect life God demands of His children. Salvation had to be paid for by Jesus and then given to us freely. 1 Peter 1:18–21 says, "For you know that it was not with perishable things such as silver and gold that you were redeemed from the empty way of life ... but with the precious blood of Christ ... Through [whom] you believe in God, who raised Him from the dead and glorified Him, and so your faith and hope are in God."

The crosses we carry in this life are much lighter and easier to bear in light of the very real cross Christ carried, was nailed to, and died on. Our crosses are lighter because we trust the crucified and risen Christ is with us, assuring that no cross we carry is forever.

As we make our way through this life, we live under the blessings Christ delivers to us through His Spirit. The Holy Spirit comes to us in Baptism, God's written Word, and the Lord's Supper. God's chief goal is for us to join Christ in heaven with praise and thanksgiving. We set our family, business, social, and recreational goals by what pleases God on account of our gratitude for the salvation Jesus earned for us on the cross. By God's Word and with the Holy Spirit's help, we rejoice in making God's goals our goals!

Heavenly Father

Please remind me every day that Your goals for my life are greater than any goals I can possibly have for myself. Thank You for sending Jesus to accomplish the greatest goal—my salvation—so I can live with a grateful heart in service to You. In Jesus' name. Amen.

Today's Challenge

As you think about the goals you wish to accomplish, ask God for His guidance. Ask Him to conform your goals to His.

Minds Ready for Action

I think the most exciting part of an action movie is when the hero is getting ready for his assault on the enemy. As music helps build the tension, the hero packs his gear, assembles his weapons, checks his ammo, goes over the plan of attack with his colleagues, and finally breaks the meeting with a rousing "Let's do it!" In the Scripture reading for today, God tells us to prepare our minds for battle. Although the weapons we use are quite different from those in an action movie, our spiritual weapons are just as effective against a far more dangerous enemy. St. Peter wrote:

> Therefore, prepare your minds for action; be self-controlled; set your hope fully on the grace to be given you when Jesus Christ is revealed. As obedient children, do not conform to the evil desires you had when you lived in ignorance. But just as He who called you is holy, so be holy in all you do.
>
> *1 Peter 1:13–15*

What takes more strength: Remaining silent while someone ridicules you or ridiculing back? Cheating on your spouse or fleeing from sexual temptations? Getting sleep on Sunday mornings or getting to church with your wife and children?

Clearly, it takes a great amount of strength to live as a child of God. The right decisions we make flow from the faith God gave us when we were baptized in His name.

Having had our sins washed away in the floodwaters of Baptism, we are born to listen and follow God's Word for the rest of our lives.

There is both an immediate and future aspect to getting our minds ready for action. Self-control is an immediate aspect and it requires great measures of strength. The future is to "set your hope fully on the grace to be given you when Jesus Christ is revealed." Both are interconnected, yet how can we accomplish either?

The same God who instructs us also supplies us with the strength needed to carry out the instructions. The Law of God commands us to, "Be holy, because [God is] holy" (1 Peter 1:16).

This is an impossible, but absolutely real, command that comes with threats of eternal condemnation for all who cannot keep it. If the Law was all we had, we would soon give up trying to be holy and fall into despair. Because the world chooses to grapple with the fear of death on its own without God, people struggle to make sense or meaning out of life and death, good and evil, and other related issues.

Thanks be to God that the Law is *not* the only thing we have to set our minds on. When our Lord Jesus Christ came to rescue us, He fulfilled the Law and used the most lethal weapon possible to defeat our eternal enemies (sin, death, and the power of the devil). St. Peter wrote, "The precious blood of Christ, a lamb without blemish or defect. He was chosen before the creation of the world, but was revealed in these last times for your sake. Through Him you believe in God, who raised Him from the dead and glorified Him, so your faith and hope are in God" (1 Peter 1:19–21). Because God chose Jesus to save us all by His very real suffering and death, we need no other evidence to confess God's love for us.

Knowing Jesus as our Savior is eternal life. Because Jesus' death and resurrection proclaims God has lovingly set His mind on us, we are inspired to faithfully keep our hearts and minds focused on His everlasting grace.

As we go to work and our children go to school, Jesus sends us out into the world "like sheep among wolves" (Matthew 10:16). Yet our Lord would not do this without first equipping us. God gave us and our families His Son, His Holy Spirit, His angels, His Word, and His means of grace. We are ready with Jesus to fight our enemies. God, through Jesus and the Holy Spirit, has made us ready for action.

Heavenly Father

When I feel more accepting of the sinful things of this world than I ought, please forgive me. Strengthen me by Your Spirit to focus my heart and mind on Christ crucified for me. In my Baptism, wash me daily to live for You. In Jesus' name. Amen.

Today's Challenge

When life's frustrations threaten to get you down, remember that things of this world are only temporary, but life in heaven is eternal.

Read Psalm 94
1 Peter 4:12–19

Stay on Course

Anyone who travels a long distance should be keenly aware of the skills of navigation. Living amid the large, rolling hills of west-central Wisconsin, one can become easily lost as the hills begin to all look alike. I speak from experience. Once I was leading an entourage of church members into these Wisconsin hills for a sleigh ride. I became so lost, I had to turn around and follow a parishioner who thankfully knew the way.

In our life as children of God, we face countless obstacles set up to distract and stop us from reaching our heavenly home. The largest obstacles are the sufferings thrown at us by the devil, this sinful world, and our own sinful flesh. In today's lesson, St. Peter acknowledges these obstacles, responding with this message: "Stay on course! Our final destination will be well worth the struggle!" Peter wrote:

> However, if you suffer as a Christian, do not be ashamed, but praise God that you bear that name. For it is time for judgment to begin with the family of God; and if it begins with us, what will the outcome be for those who do not obey the gospel of God? And, "If it is hard for the righteous to be saved, what will become of the ungodly and the sinner?" So then, those who suffer according to God's will should commit themselves to their faithful Creator and continue to do good.
>
> *1 Peter 4:16–19*

You may not be inclined to think of suffering and glory as going hand in hand. Everyone knows that a loser suffers defeat while the victor revels in earthly glory. The weak suffer and the strong enjoy worldly glory. But, as He often does, God turns this logic around. Our Lord Jesus Christ came into our world to take our suffering, our weakness, and our defeats upon Himself. Through His perfect life, and then through His innocent suffering and death on the cross, Jesus destroyed the curse of death and His suffering made God's love glorious. When you have faith in Christ, you get to trust that your suffering with the Lord affirms your faithfulness as Jesus' disciple and also glorifies your heavenly Father.

Being a baptized child of God means bearing the marks of Christ in our life. These include living a righteous life by the power of the Holy Spirit, loving God above all things, and loving all other people as much as we love ourselves. Another mark is enduring suffering for the sake of Jesus.

When Peter wrote to the churches of his day, the persecutions were just getting underway. After Peter's death, the Roman Emperor Nero falsely blamed Christians for a massive fire in Rome. Nero punished Christians by impaling them on poles, dousing them with oil, lighting them on fire, and using them as street lights. Other Christians were thrown to the wild beasts in the Coliseum. Yet notice the words God directs to these suffering Christians, "If you suffer as a Christian, do not be ashamed, but praise God that you bear that name."

The battle is fierce and we pray that we will remain faithfully on course! Faithful feeding on God's Word and the Lord's Supper in regular weekly worship is essential for you, your wife, and your children. You need every ounce of strength God gives you by His Holy Spirit for the spiritual battle rages on.

Stay on course. Put on the armor of faith, bearing the marks of Christ's suffering for our sake.

Lord Jesus

It helps to know ahead of time that sorrow and suffering are my glory in this life as I suffer for the sake of Your name. On both good and bad days, remind me that Your love guarantees me a place in Your heavenly home. In Your name. Amen.

Today's Challenge

Type out this personalized phrase from today's lesson, "The Spirit of glory and of God rests on me." Keep it close by. When you suffer on account of Jesus' name, read it and be encouraged that you are giving glory to God for Jesus' sake!

—————

I Want to Live Forever

The desire to live forever is nothing new. The Egyptian pharaohs built incredible tombs, equipped with living servants and animals to keep them company after death. The selling of one's soul to the devil in exchange for immortality is a familiar theme in folklore and storytelling.

What used to be unbelievable stories of immortality are now becoming reality as modern advancements in medical technology continue to develop ways to temporarily cheat death. In today's lesson, St. John the apostle warns us against loving the life of this world too much. John also shares words of joy and encouragement, explaining that children of God will actually live forever. John wrote:

> Do not love the world or anything in the world. If anyone loves the world, the love of the Father is not in Him. For everything in the world—the cravings of sinful man, the lust of his eyes and the boasting of what he has and does—comes not from the Father but from the world. The world and its desires pass away, but the man who does the will of God lives forever
>
> *1 John 2:15–17*

John's message to us today is simply, "Do not love the world or anything in the world." Simple to say, but difficult to do. It is hard not to love the things of this world. God's creation is wonderful, filled with fantastic things to enjoy.

When the Bible instructs us not to love the world, it is not saying that we can't enjoy the many blessings God gives to us on earth. Instead, it is warning us against following our sinful desire to allow things or people on earth to take priority over God in our hearts.

As John said, we are a hurtful and boastful people. John cautions us that when anything or anyone takes the number one position in our lives over Jesus, we commit idolatry and head down the road that takes us away from God and back toward death. But faith *in Christ* keeps God at the center of our lives.

God has prepared a life for us that will last forever. John said, "The world and its desires pass away, but the man who does the will of God lives forever." One might think this means that we can earn our way to heaven, but it doesn't. John explained exactly what it means to do the will of God as he wrote, "And this is His command: to believe in the name of His Son, Jesus Christ, and to love one another as He commanded us" (1 John 3:23).

I pray that you believe beyond all doubt that you are saved by God's grace alone, through faith alone for Christ's sake, without any merit or worthiness in you.

What we believe concerning our Lord Jesus Christ and how we live are inseparable, but understanding their relationship is crucial. Through the means of grace, the Holy Spirit creates saving faith in the hearts of those who have been baptized, communed, or who have listened to the Word of God. By such faith, God empowers us to live the Christian life according to His will.

At the end of the passage, John shows us what the Christian life is all about. He wrote, "And now, dear children, continue in Him, so that when He appears we may be confident and unashamed before Him at His coming. If you know that He is righteous, you know that everyone who does what is right has been born of Him" (1 John 2:28–29).

Trusting that we have eternal life through Jesus alone, we live the life God has always intended for us to live. The Holy Spirit is at work in our hearts through our Baptism, daily drowning the worldly, materialistic desires of the Old Adam so a new child of God may arise within us.

Since our faith and life are strengthened every time we come to worship, we continue in God's holy ways by hearing His Word and dining at His table, rejoicing that we are already living forever in Christ!

Dear Heavenly Father

I rejoice that am living with You forever! Thank You for purchasing my eternal life through the precious blood of Your only Son. Remind me by Your Spirit's power every day that I belong to You now and am dead to sin for Jesus' sake. In Jesus' name. Amen.

Today's Challenge

Every time you have to have maintenance performed on your car, house, or boat, remember that the things of this world will pass away. Rejoice that Your home in heaven will never pass away!

Read Psalm 98
1 John 3:1–10

Lavished with Love

Maybe you have played that little game with your wife when you say "I love you," and she responds, "I love you *more.*" Then you say, "No, *I* love *you* more." And so on, and so on.

Imagine this contest with God! That would be like trying to see who could get each other wetter. Imagine that you had a fire hose with 150 pounds of pressure shooting straight up into the sky. But God could bring down a tidal wave that would flow over you, submerging you and all else.

Perhaps this is an unusual analogy, but when it comes to the question of who loves who more, God will always win because He lost His Son on the cross. For us, being a loser has never felt so good. The waters of Baptism have covered us and we have been lavished with God's love. John wrote:

> How great is the love the Father has lavished on us, that we should be called children of God! And that is what we are! The reason the world does not know us is that it did not know Him. Dear friends, now we are children of God, and what we will be has not yet been made known. But we know that when He appears, we shall be like Him, for we shall see Him as He is. Everyone who has this hope in Him purifies himself, just as He is pure.
>
> *1 John 3:1–3*

At this point in John's life, the early church was enduring great persecution—especially from those in the Roman Empire—for bearing the name of Christ. Since the Christians refused to offer incense to Caesar (a form of worship to the emperor), the government found them guilty of treason. Treason was punishable by death. John explains the cruel actions of the world saying, "The reason the world does not know us is that it did not know Him."

John then encourages those of every generation—beginning with his own—to remain faithful to the Lord who revealed His love for us through the cross. John wrote, "Dear friends, now we are children of God, and what we will be has not yet been made known. But we know that when He appears, we shall be like Him, for we shall see Him as He is."

If we want to know what we will be like the day our Lord Jesus returns, we can look to Jesus' resurrection on Easter morning. St. John was at the open tomb and believed that Jesus was the risen Savior of the world. John also saw the Lord alive, following His resurrection, with real bones and skin, but glorified unlike any human being. John testified, "Then [Jesus] said to Thomas, 'Put your finger here; see My hands. Reach out your hand and put it into My side. Stop doubting and believe.' Thomas said to Him, 'My Lord and my God!'" (John 20:27–28).

We too shall rise again with glorified bodies on the day He returns with great power and glory accompanied by countless angels.

Since God has lavished us with eternal love as revealed in His Son's death and resurrection, John directs our focus to the here and now. He wrote, "Everyone who has this hope in Him purifies himself, just as He is pure. ... Dear children, do not let anyone lead you astray. He who does what is right is righteous, just as [God] is righteous. He who does what is sinful is of the devil, because the devil has been sinning from the beginning. The reason the Son of God appeared was to destroy the devil's work" (1 John 3:3–8).

God has already given us eternal life. God wants us to trust that life has already begun in this world so we can live as the children He has made us to be in Christ. Since our wives and children are just as precious to God as we are, God calls us to lead them to the life-giving Word and the faith-strengthening benefits of the Lord's Supper in worship. Growing in the confidence that we are children of God, we rejoice, knowing that God always loves us *more*. Let us share His tidal wave of love with everyone we meet!

Heavenly Father

I am grateful for how You have lavished Your eternal love upon me at the expense of Your only Son's blessed life. Strengthen me by Your Spirit to live a grateful life to Your glory until I see You face-to-face in heaven. In Jesus' name. Amen.

Today's Challenge

Enjoy the love you have received from your heavenly Father and lavish it on your wife, children, and anyone else who can benefit from God's abundant love through Christ. That includes everyone!

Read Psalm 30
1 John 5:1–5

A Command We'll Want to Obey

I was five and it was Thanksgiving Day. The Minnesota Gopher fight song was playing on the television. The smells of homemade stuffing, mashed potatoes, and spiced apples in Grandpa and Grandma Gall's home competed with the rich aroma of a turkey whose time in the oven was nearly over. All around were the sounds of well-orchestrated cooking. I was commanded to stay out of the kitchen, but my weak and hungry flesh made it very tough to obey. There was one command, however, I couldn't wait to obey. Soon Grandma would order us to come and eat.

God has also issued a command we'll want to obey. John wrote:

> Everyone who believes that Jesus is the Christ is born of God, and everyone who loves the Father loves His Child as well. This is how we know that we love the children of God: by loving God and carrying out His commands.
>
> *1 John 5:1–2*

God gave us the Ten Commandments as the perfect rule for Christian living. However, because human beings are not perfect, we cannot keep the Ten Commandments. We're too sinful to follow all of them on our own. That is why God had to step in and win our salvation for us. Romans 5:6 says, "You see, at just the right time, when we were still powerless, Christ died for the ungodly."

When Jesus came to earth, He kept God's Ten Commandments perfectly in our place. By His innocent suffering and death, He satisfied God's just anger over our sin. Romans 6:23 says, "For the wages of sin is death, but the gift of God is eternal life in Christ Jesus our Lord."

By Jesus' death and resurrection, He has gained for *us* the victory over sin, death, and the power of the devil. We no longer need to fear these enemies. John reveals how we can express our fearlessness by saying, "This is love for God: to obey His commands. And His commands are not burdensome, for everyone born of God overcomes the world. This is the victory that has overcome the world, even our faith. Who is it that overcomes the world? Only he who believes that Jesus is the Son of God" (1 John 5:3–5).

Through faith in Christ, God grants us confidence to live without fear of being His children and to obey His invitation to join in the celebration of Him overcoming the world. I think of Grandma's command to come and eat. We, of course, could not wait to participate in the meal she had prepared. As we come to worship around God's Word and sacraments, we participate in the banquet feast God has already prepared for us in this life. And this weekly feast prepares us for God's eternal banquet feast in heaven. Everything has been prepared for you!

Let's take a moment to focus once again on what John writes, "Everyone who loves the Father loves His Child as well. This is how we know that we love the children of God: by loving God and carrying out His commands. This is love for God: to obey His commands." John uses the image of family to illustrate that everyone who loves God the Father will love His children as well. It is God's love in us, strengthened through faith in Christ, that enables us to love Him above all things and demonstrate His love to others—a command we'll want to obey for Jesus' sake!

Heavenly Father

Your love for me is rich in eternal life and joys that have no end. Strengthen me with Your Holy Spirit so I may obey Your commands. In Jesus' name. Amen.

Today's Challenge

If you know someone who is trying to earn their way to heaven, share with them the Good News of the Gospel. Jesus has overcome the world. Through Him we have eternal life.

Tears? What Tears?

I have a memory from when I was five. I was in the hospital for a hernia surgery. Between my parents' faithful visits, I was homesick and shed quite a few tears. Once a nurse walked in while I was crying, and I was embarrassed. Thinking fast, I told her I was getting a drink and water sprayed up in my face. As a grown man, I now realize that not many people like to be caught crying, *especially* men. In our devotion for today, we find that God has plans for us that will forever put an end to tears of sadness and pain. St. John wrote:

> And he said, "These are they who have come out of the great tribulation; they have washed their robes and made them white in the blood of the Lamb. Therefore, they are before the throne of God and serve Him day and night in His temple; and He who sits on the throne will spread His tent over them. Never again will they hunger; never again will they thirst. The sun will not beat upon them, nor any scorching heat. For the Lamb at the center of the throne will be their Shepherd; He will lead them to springs of living water. And God will wipe away every tear from their eyes."
>
> *Revelation 7:14–17*

God's Word is precious. God the Holy Spirit inspired 46 different human writers over a span of nearly 1,600 years to write a complete library of 66 books that speak consistently and without error the message of our salvation in Jesus Christ. The last book of the Bible, the Revelation of St. John, is a fitting conclusion to this library because it reveals how God, through Christ, will tie together our whole salvation history.

Today's lesson from Revelation chapter seven tells what our loved ones who have left this vale of tears on earth experience in heaven. Our departed loved ones are among the great company of saints (all believers in Christ), and we too shall be numbered with them when we arrive in heaven. Our greatest joy on that wonderful day will be to stand before the throne and in front of the Lamb. The Lamb is our Lord Jesus Christ "who takes away the sin of the world" (John 1:29).

This vision God gave John is dripping with the Good News of salvation in Christ. John wrote, "These are they who have come out of the great tribulation; they have washed their robes and made them white in the blood of the Lamb." A person doesn't earn this! This is purely God's work! Through faith our sins are washed clean in the blessed flood of the Lamb's blood, shed for us on the cross.

Through our Baptism, this washing has been personally delivered to us along with the gift of our saving faith. Through the Sacrament of the Altar, we eat and drink the same body and blood Christ gave up for us on the cross for the forgiveness of our sins and the strengthening of that faith.

Gathering faithfully each week with our wives and children in worship, we joyfully anticipate the day of resurrection. On that day, we will stand with palm branches in hand, clothed in sinless bodies, singing that glorious song, "Salvation belongs to our God, who sits on the throne, and to the Lamb. ... Amen! Praise and glory and wisdom and thanks and honor and power and strength be to our God for ever and ever. Amen!" (Revelation 7:10–12).

If we have plenty of things to cry about in this life, we can look forward to the Last Day when we will be able to say, "Tears? What tears? Only tears of joy!"

Blessed Is Your Name Forever, O Lamb of God, Jesus Christ!

By the power of the Holy Spirit in Baptism, You have already washed my robe and made it white through Your blood shed for me on the cross. Help me walk in humble faith before You all my days until I stand before Your glorious throne with all the angels and saints in Your Kingdom forever! In Your holy name. Amen.

Today's Challenge

Next time you feel like crying, go ahead. Just remember, tears of pain and sadness are only temporary and will not exist in heaven, where there will only be tears of joy!

Read Psalm 119 (89–96)
Revelation 22:1–21

Getting Back to Eden

How many commercials or comedy skits have depicted Adam and Eve in the Garden of Eden? Often the story of Adam and Eve is performed in a humorous, belittling way, seeming to imply that the story is little more than a mythical tale.

Today's reading hearkens us back to the events recorded in the first three chapters of Genesis—true and historical. As we turn to the last book of the Bible, we see how important it is that we believe the Genesis account of God creating a perfect world for us in the beginning. We see that after Adam and Eve fell into sin, God never forgot about His promise to bring us to a new Eden—our perfect home in heaven. St. John wrote:

> Then the angel showed me the river of the water of life, as clear as crystal, flowing from the throne of God and of the Lamb down the middle of the great street of the city. On each side of the river stood the tree of life, bearing twelve crops of fruit, yielding its fruit every month. And the leaves of the tree are for the healing of the nations. No longer will there be any curse. The throne of God and of the Lamb will be in the city, and His servants will serve Him. They will see His face, and His name will be on their foreheads.
>
> *Revelation 22:1–4*

God had told Adam and Eve, "You are free to eat from any tree in the garden; but you must not eat from the tree of the knowledge of good and evil, for when you eat of it you will surely die" (Genesis 2:16–17).

When our first parents were seduced by the devilish serpent, they brought God's curse upon this earth. The worst consequence of this curse was eternal death in hell. Immediately, God went to work saving us. To the serpent He said, "I will put enmity between you and the woman, and between your offspring and hers; He will crush your head, and He will strike your heel" (Genesis 3:15).

God banished Adam and Eve from the Garden of Eden in their state of sinfulness so they would not eat of the tree of life, for that would mean living eternally in sin.

God executed His promise for salvation that would lead to an eternity without sin—an eternity with Him in heaven. This promise was fulfilled through the blood of the Lamb on the cross to pay for the guilt, the curse, and the eternal punishment our sins had brought upon us.

Through Christ alone we come to the tree of life waiting for us in heaven. Could the scene John pictured of our new Eden—our heavenly Home—be any more perfect? Driving Adam and Eve out of Eden was an expression of God's justice and compassionate love. God wanted the entire human race to eat the fruit of the tree of life, with perfect bodies washed clean in the precious blood of His Son.

As husbands and fathers, faith in Christ is all the motivation needed for taking our families to worship every week! Trusting God's promise inspires us to lead the dearest people in our lives to the arms of Jesus through Baptism, God's Holy Word, and Jesus' true body and blood in the Lord's Supper. We have God's surest pledge, sealed in the blood of Christ, that the Holy Spirit will preserve within our hearts saving faith in Christ.

As we feed on the means of grace, we live in hope and expectation, trusting that we will stand together on the Last Day for Jesus' sake. Then, with all our loved ones before the throne of Christ, we will reach out our hand and eat from the tree of life and drink from the river of the water of life flowing from God's throne. Our present trials are indeed worth bearing, for God is bringing us to a new Eden!

Oh Father, Son, and Holy Spirit, Blessed Trinity

Thank You for never giving up on us. Preserve us in the true faith of our Lord Jesus crucified and risen until we see You face-to-face! In Jesus' name. Amen.

Today's Challenge

Read Bible stories with your family on a routine basis, designating a regular reading time once a day or once a week. Discuss with your children how these Bible stories point to Christ and were part of God's plan for our salvation. Thank God for the gracious gift of His Word.